# DAUGHTERS
# OF CHANGE

# DAUGHTERS OF CHANGE

## Growing Up Female in America

## Janet Chase

Little, Brown and Company     Boston/Toronto

FIRST EDITION

Quiz from *Young People and A.A.* reprinted with permission of A.A. World Services, Inc.

LIBRARY OF CONGRESS CATALOGING IN PUBLICATION DATA

Chase, Janet.
Daughters of change.

Bibliography: p.
1. Daughters—United States. 2. Mothers and daughters. 3. Adolescent girls. I. Title.
HQ777.C53      305.2'3      81-3787      3. Adolescence -
ISBN 0-316-13820-7      AACR2                4. Girls.

MV

Designed by Susan Windheim

*Published simultaneously in Canada by Little, Brown & Company (Canada) Limited*

PRINTED IN THE UNITED STATES OF AMERICA

## *Dedication*

To my parents who raised me with love and pride. Like many children, at one time or another, I was angry at them for failing to teach me everything I thought I needed to know to make my life easy and comfortable.

I am now convinced that growing up — and God knows, to everyone's pain, adolescence can seem to last forever — means no longer being obliged to blame your family for the part of you that never got to be prom queen, the part that is still sometimes frightened and unsure of what is right, the part that would rather cling to the familiar than risk the unknown.

And I am sure that the most precious gift parents and children — and we are all each other's parents and children — can give one another is to simply allow the other to be exactly who they are. To do that, it is essential to learn to look past the disguises we wear, disguises variously called parent and child, husband and wife, boss, friend, lover, and so on. Only then do we see the beauty that is unfailingly there.

That is something of what I try to do here.

Marion and Hank, I love you.

Growth:
The perplexity of a mind and a heart
Not comprehending — but somehow
Knowing,
I am like a rose.
Full grown, petals open . . .
But not yet ready.
I am like a pearl . . .
Still Unformed.
But I have begun.
And I will become.

*— Janet Chase, age 14.*

# Contents

# DAUGHTERS
# OF CHANGE

# *Introduction*

OUR DAUGHTERS ARE IN TROUBLE, and more loudly than ever before, they are telling us about their despondency, their isolation, their reluctance to grow up to meet a world in which the ground rules — especially for women — are so uncertain. And while they may not be able to make known in so many words exactly where it hurts, their message is coming across with painful eloquence.

Last year, for instance, approximately 300,000 adolescent girls attempted suicide — three times as many girls as boys. And for the first time, girls are beginning to catch up to boys in "successful" suicides, so that they now make up 40 percent of adolescent suicides. In the past, girls have chosen rather passive methods of self-destruction, but now, instead of swallowing a handful of Mother's Valium, a growing number are opting for "masculine" ways out — like jumping from heights, hanging themselves, and stabbing themselves through the heart.

As an HEW official pronounces tersely: "The current cultural shift toward blurring of the sex roles has contributed to the problem."

And while the much-touted teenage sexual revolution has, in actuality, been one in which the flesh has indeed been more than willing but the spirit has lagged far behind, there has been enormous fallout from the increase in sexual activity.

Consider: Despite the relative availability of contraceptives, more than a million girls, most unmarried, will become pregnant this year. If the trend continues, an Alan Guttmacher Institute spokesman projects that "a staggering 42 percent of all girls will have been pregnant by the time they reach twenty." Almost one-fourth will have borne at least one child — most of those who keep their babies will drop out of school and never return. Thirteen percent will have had at least one abortion.

Girls are moving up the criminal ladder at breakneck speed; the total arrest rate for juvenile girls is twice eclipsing the increase for boys. In the last fifteen years, according to FBI records, arrests of girls under eighteen rose 500 percent for violent crimes and 400 percent for possession of firearms and crimes against property.

Some of our daughters are starving themselves — some to achieve an uncompromising ideal of feminine perfection — some to death. Some are turning to prostitution. Countless numbers run away from home, sending back brief — desperate, angry — report cards from roadside telephone booths.

Of course, despite the alarming statistics, most young women are not grabbing headlines with their pain. Some simply become more subdued, or don't seem to have as many friends as they used to. There may be uncomfortable silences when they are in the room, where before the laughter was easy. They may stay out until three A.M., or they may not leave the house at all.

Many may seem to be doing just fine, fitting into none

of the alarming categories above. "Thank God," you breathe with relief, "none of that is happening to my daughter. Or to me." And the fact is that your daughter, given the percentages, does stand a good chance of making it through her adolescence relatively unscathed.

And still you read the newspapers, and you wonder, is your daughter one of the nation's six million "sexually active" teens? If she is, is she protecting herself physically — and emotionally? Are her mood swings, the abrupt flashes of anger and the fits of crying, dictated by drugs? Does she think about harming herself?

The men and women who study and counsel our daughters are concerned about the number of casualties they are seeing. What is going wrong? Doesn't this new crop of young women have more to look forward to than any previous generation had? They have new careers open to them. They have the promise of relationships based not on sexual role playing, but on equality and mutual respect. They have liberation from social ills of every hue, from stifling sex roles to sexual hang-ups.

And while it is true that there have never been greater possibilities of more open doors for women, this is not a charmed age in which to grow up female. Though history for women is indeed being rewritten, there are few role models and no new systems of values to tell them how to get by in this brave new world.

Parents often encourage their daughters — in ways formerly reserved for male children — to "make something of" themselves, as if who they *are* is not enough. Some of us are adding another frightening message: "We didn't have the chances you have, so do what we were not able to." It is difficult enough to "do it" for ourselves; it is a burden to do it for others.

Adolescents, regardless of gender, are feeling other pressures. As a society, we no longer seem to believe in setting long-range goals. "Do it now," "Be here now" seem to be much more popular philosophies these days. Since adolescence — the *Happy Days* situation-comedy mystique aside — is not generally marked by happy times, if a teen is not getting what she wants out of life right now, she feels there is little promise of something better coming along tomorrow. And she may strike out as if there *were* no tomorrow.

Psychologists and sociologists also believe that we may be doing a grave disservice to our young people with all of the emphasis we are placing on "doing one's own thing," a philosophy that has evolved, at least in part, because we have become so wary of depending on others, even on our families. "We have become very egocentric and competitive — even with our own children," says a psychologist who has a teenage daughter. "Our traditional resources — family, church, schools, government — are seen as untruthful and untrustworthy." So in a world where Mom and Dad are both working, and grandparents are off living the good life in some retirement city, whom can teenagers depend on but themselves? That's just not enough.

We have been pummeled with so many conflicting views of the "right way" to raise a family that we have become afraid of our own children. Either we are unwilling to venture across any real or imagined generation gaps to talk about morals and values with our daughters, or we storm across with a barrage of commandments, and lose them that way. We are not even sure that we *want* to know if they are taking drugs, if they are having sex. We are afraid to know them as people.

This book is not meant to be a sociological horror story,

and it is not primarily about those girls whose crises have reached certifiably tragic proportions. And this is not a traditional child-rearing book, for there are no magic formulas or absolutes herein. I don't believe there are such things, and it gets in the way to pretend there are.

Neither is this a book about blaming or guilt. If there is something missing from your relationship with your daughter, it is not really helpful to spend much time wondering if you have "done it wrong." I know that if you are taking the time to read this, you must care about your daughter, and perhaps want something more rewarding with her and for her.

What is this then? This is a true story — a collection of true stories — about what it is like growing up female today, and this also is a book about having a warm, loving "relationship" with your teenage daughter. In this age of gropings for sensitivity and high-tech spiritual enlightenment, I have to admit that I feel a little sheepish talking about "relationships" — a fragile concept that has, of late, been worn into the ground. What do I mean, then, by that word? I'll start by reaching back beyond the era of encounter, to the dictionary. Relationship, *Webster's* tells us, is a connection, an association, an involvement, an affinity, a kinship. That's a good place to start.

An important part of having a relationship with your daughter includes seeing her as a separate being, as a soul who is related to you, but who exists outside of your personal mirror. It means acknowledging her as a sexual being (which does not at all mean being crazy about the idea of her having sex) and as a spiritual being. It means helping her to determine the goals, the values, the reality that are right for her.

In the following chapters, I will look into the nature of

liberation and how our sometimes peculiar ideas about it manifest themselves in our daughters as certain "symptoms" — symptoms that include loneliness and depression — that in too many cases lead to suicidal gestures, drug and alcohol use and abuse, and very early sexuality and pregnancy.

I will also discuss the meaning of sexuality to girls and to their mothers, its emotional and physical consequences, and how our changing morals, values, and goals are influencing young women. I'll examine what your daughter may really be trying to say when she takes drugs or when she has sex, and describe the symptoms of depression that can lead to suicide or thought of suicide.

And while there are no foolproof solutions, I do offer some ideas, suggestions, alternatives. I will, of course, also delve into the delicate and complex nature of the relationship between mother and teenage daughter in these changing times.

This is a confusing time for all women, certainly not least of all for the women who are mothers. The questions you may be considering, and the questions the women I interviewed have certainly considered, include: How are mothers supposed to relate to their supposedly liberated daughters? What do teenage girls want from their mothers? What do you have to give your daughter? And what do you want from her?

In many books on parenting, much of the person who happens to be the parent seems to get lost. I think it is really important to talk about how it *feels* to live with and be responsible for the growth of a child — or a young woman. What about the frustrations you feel as a citizen of a society whose exterior trappings, at least, seem to be so sexually open? Are you jealous of your daughter because she stands to reap the windfalls of liberation? I don't want this book to forget that there is much more than a parent inside of every mother.

We are also citizens of the age of the expert — a group whose numbers crowd bookstore shelves and television talk shows. I am not one of those. I don't have a degree that qualifies me to sew people together when they are torn apart. Nor do I yet have any children of my own. So why should *I* have written this book? I am a journalist who writes about people, and I have talked extensively both to those who work with teenage girls and their families and to mothers and daughters who have grown up together, or who are in the process of doing so. None of them knows all of the right answers, but they try not to turn away from the questions. They have struggled, and in that struggle have become something more in the eyes of the other.

I can't say whether I will ever have a daughter; I know I would like one — especially after researching and writing this book. Regardless, the relationships between young women and their mothers (and with other people who care for and are concerned about them) have always been very significant to me. Currently, I inhabit a space in time and circumstance between the teenage daughter and the mother. And because I am no longer committed to one role nor yet caught up in the other, I have stood aside and observed how many mothers and daughters fail to see the special beauty in each other. And I have also been caught up in the joy they shared.

This book serves another purpose for me. I also write it for a scrawny, wild-haired child with dark eyes that couldn't see light. Twenty years ago, when she was twelve and her body began to show signs of somersaulting her into womanhood, she simply stopped eating. Anorexia was the name they gave it, an uncommon disease then, a near epidemic now. Being grown-up, going out in the world, it seemed to her, was too painful.

It wasn't that she didn't want to eat. She was hungry. Very hungry. But she had to stop putting life into her body in order to learn a new way to live.

It was easy for people to feel uncomfortable around her; she was cranky and pitiable and she reminded them of things they would sooner forget. And for a long time she refused to respond to their cajoling and threats to eat. Most could not understand what she was trying to say. But a few saw beauty in her. "There is sunlight coming from you," someone said. "Feel it."

It took a whole dark winter and part of the spring, but finally she did. She grew up to be a strong woman who is still sometimes a child with dark eyes that strain to see light. But, then, sometimes she sees that she is a brilliant jewel, a shining star.

I am that child and that woman. The two of us have had a relationship that has become more comfortable, more accepting, more loving over the years. I would like other girls to see their inner brilliance, and I want mothers and daughters to learn more about the beauty within each other. This is a book for them, and for all others who want to have relationships with them.

And this is also for those who strain to see perfection when it is invisible.

# 1

## *The Price of Freedom*

SHE HAD IT ALL. Or so it seemed.

If we still believed in fairy tales, she would get the role of the princess. She — Laura — was sixteen and promising to be beautiful, although at her age the promise was scarcely enough to satisfy her. She was also kind and generous, and while she stayed far enough in the background to disqualify herself from winning any adolescent popularity contests, Laura had her share of friends.

She was smart, smart enough to be put in accelerated classes, although she had to work harder than most of her classmates to keep up. She had the brightest of futures ahead of her, especially since she was lucky enough, as her mother kept reminding her, to be coming of age in a time when everyone agreed that women were free to do anything — or almost anything — that men could do.

Nancy, Laura's mother, had grown up in another, less enchanted time. In what by now must be considered a sociological cliché, years ago Nancy had quit college to support her new husband through law school. And though the agreement was that as soon as Tom graduated, Nancy would go back to school to finish her degree in social work, by the time he was studying for his state bar exams, Nancy was pregnant with Laura. And then with Laura's two brothers.

So Nancy put her own life on the back burner and quietly began pinning her dreams on her only daughter. Laura would not have to limit herself to social work — at home or anywhere else. "Laura can be an astronaut, a doctor, the president of a corporation," Nancy would brag to her friends. "Times are different now — there are no obstacles in *her* way."

But dreams are seldom transferrable, intact and undiminished, from one generation to another. Laura was scared she wasn't up to fulfilling her mother's dream, and she wasn't at all sure of what her own dreams were.

So, at age sixteen, Laura of the shimmering promises met a boy who told her she was beautiful — beautiful right now and not at some future, unknowable time. Laura was flattered when the boy said she made him feel like a man, and even though she was a little disappointed that she didn't suddenly feel like a woman, she was somehow relieved when she found she was pregnant.

Now all of the dreams — her own and her mother's — wouldn't have to be tested and found to be lacking under the weight of reality.

Tom and Nancy — especially Nancy — were hurt and angry. Somewhere, something had gone very wrong, though they couldn't figure out what they had done. And Nancy found herself feeling absolutely betrayed when Laura announced, shakily but with certainty, that she would keep and raise her baby.

"That girl is throwing everything away," her mother

raged. "She had it all and she doesn't want any of it. Can you believe that?"

"She had it all, and she doesn't want it." We had better believe that, because countless young women like Laura are telling us in painful, wordless communiqués — by becoming pregnant, by using and abusing drugs and alcohol, by running away from home, by going on sometimes fatal hunger strikes called anorexia, by taking their lives in other ways — that sometimes having "all of it" isn't nearly enough.

These are not the simplest of times for any of us. And yet we try to convince our daughters that they have everything they need to be happy. What, after all, do they lack? Not only do the material things come easy to them — courtesy of our struggles — but the promise of a grand liberation is there for the plucking. Isn't it?

It is with the most loving intentions that parents are telling their daughters, "For you, life will be different." Yet, in reality, we are handing them the same old cherished ideas that security and assurance are products of external circumstances — getting the right people, the right jobs, the right degrees into our lives. And, all the time, the statistics keep right on saying that those things, *by themselves,* don't bring genuine satisfaction and freedom.

One lovely young woman who has not yet shown up in the endless parade of statistics might be speaking for a whole generation of girls.

"People are always telling me I should be *this*. Then they say I should be *that*. 'Aren't I lucky to be growing up now?' When they aren't telling me those things, I have voices in my head telling me the same things. 'Get ahead.'

'Be somebody.' 'Do something with your life.' All I hear
are 'shoulds.'

"You know what I feel like? A pincushion. There is an
awful lot of pushing going on. You push, they push, and
when you finally get someplace, you realize there isn't all
that much there.

"Don't tell anybody I said it, but there are lots of times
I wish I was still a child and all people expected of me was
to be cute."

In part, this book is about how difficult, and how exciting, it is to be growing up female today. In part, it is about
our confusion — society's confusion — about the nature
of happiness and freedom, and how our daughters are
catching that confusion.

Which does not mean that I do not fully support the
sort of freedom called feminism. I do, wholeheartedly. Yet
the grim statistics which bear witness to the pain felt by
young women also tell me something more is needed.

Let us begin by looking at the rewards of what we call
women's liberation. What women are only beginning to
realize, thanks to the many battles won by the feminist
movement, is a long overdue boost into the social and economic mainstream, including greater opportunity for
women to advance in many areas of endeavor, more equi-
table pay, the chance to make a statement and be heard,
and the room to define themselves on their own terms
rather than by how the other half views them.

As a result, teenage girls no longer are obligated to see
their futures tied into any one narrow idea or activity.
They are told they have new options in blending career
and family, and they are beginning to see more women as
doctors and lawyers as well as nurses and secretaries. There
is more real communication between the sexes; teenage

boys and girls are friends in many ways in which their parents probably were not.

For mothers of teenagers, the movement has offered a new sense of self and beginnings, so that they may be less likely to suffer the "empty nest" syndrome when their children learn to fly and more inclined to seek out the answers to their own questions.

All of that is good, and is lending an undeniably richer texture to the fabric of all of our lives. But something important is still missing, because in spite of all of these apparent new opportunities, we — female and male — do not seem to be a lot happier or more peaceful than we were before we had a taste of freedom from constricting sex roles, sexual inhibitions, and prohibitions against expressing emotion.

Perhaps our problem comes from the fact that we are still caught in "in between" times. The old order was sexist and confusing and unfree, while the new one is uncertain and sometimes too demanding. And the messages our daughters are receiving from every quarter more often then not contradict each other.

"We're seeing a remarkable transitional time for young women," says Cleveland psychiatrist Victor Victoroff. "More than ever before they are being encouraged to move into high-pressure careers and to be more sexually liberated. They are also getting messages that the business of raising children and maintaining a household is rather dowdy and boring, to be reserved for pinheaded women who don't have anything better to do with their lives.

"At the same time, they may be hearing a much more traditional message from their parents. The pull on these girls is enormous."

The Reverend Robert Iles, an Episcopal priest, marriage

and family counselor, and teacher of human sexuality, agrees that the task of edging into womanhood is more difficult now, in part, *because* of all the new options. "Girls have many more choices now about who they are going to be, how they will express themselves, earn their living, and relate to others.

"It's much harder to carve out an identity than it was fifteen years ago. Girls have so many divergent forces vying for their attention. They must critically evaluate what they hear from feminists like Gloria Steinem, from 'total women' like Marabel Morgan, and from their own mothers.

"And it is also more difficult being a mother today — they have no idea what they should be telling their daughters about what values are workable or how to get about in the world."

The traditional sex roles — and by no means do I suggest a return to the decidedly not-so-good old days — may, at least, have provided some stability and security to the unstable, insecure time of life called adolescence. Now that what it means to be a man or a woman is no longer set in concrete, it is more difficult for a young person to know when her idea of herself fits in with what the culture expects of her.

Girls are getting the word that all the barriers are down, that this is no longer a man's world. They can get ahead, go to the top, have it all. They can *be* somebody. The world may be their oyster, but we forgot to inform them that the pearl is not always there, or that its price is sometimes too great, for even while we tell them that they can be *anything* they want to be, we are holding back part of the truth.

By definition, liberation allows choices. It does not demand conformation to a new, albeit nobler, ethic. But that is what has happened, for the choices that the emancipation of the fairer sex was supposed to allow have been turned into compulsions and, in many instances, we have simply traded in one set of shoulds for another. Now when many of us — even dyed-in-the-wool homemakers — hear of an intelligent, even, God forbid, educated young woman who is planning to spend the years between twenty-five and forty-five largely in devotion to house, husband, and child, we shake our heads and mutter with regret, "But she *should* be *doing* something with her life."

"It's no longer good enough to be the wife of a doctor or an executive," says Peggy Golden, a therapist who counsels young women and is herself the mother of a nineteen-year-old daughter. "Smart girls — sometimes merely competent girls — are expected, all of a sudden, without rules or role models, to become doctors and captains of industry themselves."

In essence, we seem to be trying to convince our daughters that it is a sin not to shout a resounding "yes" to every opportunity that comes a-knocking. But there isn't even a semblance of liberation unless they also have the right to say, "No, thanks, I'll pass this time."

What we seem to have is a clear-cut case of off-with-the-old, on-with-the-new-itis. We are determinedly eager simply to pitch out all of our old ideas about what women should be and do and have, without questioning the meaning of either the old or the new ways.

But then it seems to me that we have always been a culture that is more interested in the broad, sweeping gestures than in the subtle half shades. So it is in character that in recent years we have painted a brave picture of feminine strength, determination, and self-reliance in bright, gaudy colors, right over the old canvas of soft mauves and pinks. For the most part, we haven't questioned whether either one without the other — or even an artful blending of both — presents a complete picture of the Whole Woman.

As a result, the social landscape is strewn with outdated expectations and crumbled stereotypes for women, young and not-so-young. What was desired feminine behavior — passivity, domestic subservience, and a capacity for never-ending nurturing — in Mother's day is fast being treated, therapeutized, and exorcised by consciousness-raising, assertion training, and affirmative action.

The old storybook rewards — a marriage that promises to live happily ever after, the security of owning a home and two cars, the praise and protection of a strong man — that we always took for granted were part and parcel of being a good woman and reproducer — are fast becoming social, economic, and psychological anachronisms.

And the new rewards continue to remain unclear. We tell our daughters, get thee a career — but when they try to, they find there aren't enough jobs that truly qualify as careers. We say a nonsexist relationship with a loving, gentle man can be yours — but where, please tell, are all those feminist dreamboats hiding? The pot of gold must still be lurking at the end of the rainbow — but which rainbow?

So, while we make blithe promises to our daughters that the world is theirs, many of these new opportunities are still in the blueprint stage. For, despite media hype and wishful thinking to the contrary, society is not yet, in the most meaningful sense, supporting the emancipation of its young women.

Consider a recent Los Angeles *Times* poll that found

that over half those surveyed believe that the "feminist movement has gone too far," while three-quarters concur that youth has too much freedom nowadays.

Or take a poll anywhere in this country and you will find that Americans, given their genetic druthers, would still have a boy over a girlchild any day.

Consider the fact that corporate foundations continue to donate four times as much money to youth agencies serving boys, while, naturally, girls are hurting for the financial slight. Those who work with girls charge that the services that *are* offered are often fragmented, sexist, and out-of-date. As Edith Phelps, executive director of Girls Clubs of America, puts it: "Agencies serving girls are still being asked to operate efficiently with a stove, a sewing machine, and a loving heart."

Consider our educational system. Despite efforts to update the legends of Dick and Jane, schools at all levels doggedly perpetuate sexist images. Textbooks pay little attention to the changing roles of man and women, and, for the most part, students are still encouraged to take sex-biased classes, and to enter sex-segregated fields of study and employment.

All of which worries educators like Bea Mayes, professor at the City University of New York. "High schools are still preparing women for a protected future that does not exist and are failing to ready them for full partnership in the wage-earning community."

Young women are not only being encouraged to chase after what are still, in many cases, rainbows, but the prevailing ethic may also be pointing them toward a dream that was never worthy of the dreaming in the first place. By that I mean our cockeyed view about the nature of freedom, the one that says that because men have always been given the green light to do more, go more, have more, they must be freer souls.

Therefore, liberation for women has sometimes been taken as synonomous with being allowed to do the things that men do. Never mind that the pile of evidence accumulated by our husbands and sons would seem to be sufficient to make women doubt that the "doing" of anything without humble understanding has little to do with freedom or happiness.

To the contrary, women have managed to ignore that little truth of life, and having earned fair and squarely the right to compete for the same dubious prizes, are going after them — and, lo and behold — coming up just as mentally and spiritually bereft.

In fact, women are even beginning to show formerly male-specific syndromes, not just career-related stress and anxiety, but ulcers, coronary disease, and hypertension.

Our daughters have also caught the belief that if males do it, it must be freedom. So, now, in our quest for the holy grail of liberation, we may be seeing what amounts to a "girls will be boys" parody. It is small wonder that an attitude that goes roughly, "I have a right to be as free sexually, to get the same highs, even to bend the same laws as boys," has become common among our daughters.

In the "old days," parents were always quick to wink at certain types of behavior — rudeness and rowdiness, disrespect and drinking, and the obligatory sowing of wild oats — in their sons, adhering fast to the old "boys will be boys" saw.

But these, we hear tell, are the "new" days. So are parents ready to accept a single standard of behavior from children of either sex? We — society, some parents — only pretend that we do, and it's the mixed messages that drive people a little nuts.

While on the one hand girls hear that they are now free to be one of the boys, with the other hand we spank them when they try. We still smile when our sons engage in the sort of behavior that proves they are real men. But real sexual equality aside, we still want our daughters to be "good girls," not "real women." We still, if not always in so many words, demand greater obedience and chastity from our girlchildren.

While the odds are in your favor that your daughter will never be stopped by the police for anything more serious than doing 40 in a 30-mile-an-hour zone, I think nothing would reveal more about our still hale-and-hearty double standard for young people than a quick look at our nation's outmoded system of juvenile justice.

While I have already briefly pointed out that violent crime has risen rapidly among young girls in the last few years, there is another sort of almost exclusively female "crime" that bears our attention. According to the National Criminal Justice Information and Statistics Service, of the million-plus teenagers who are processed through the courts every year, 70 percent of the girls (and only 23 percent of the boys) are charged with "status offenses" — infractions of the law that apply only to minors.

Such offenses include school truancy, running away from home, incorrigibility (which can mean anything from disobeying parents to curfew violations to smoking or having a "bad attitude"), using vulgar language in public, associating with immoral persons, and promiscuity.

"Truancy and incorrigibility charges against girls are often nothing more than a guise for punishing sexual behavior that would draw little more than a wink in a case involving a boy," points out John Rector, chief administrator of the Office of Juvenile Justice and Delinquency Prevention.

When he was chairman of the Senate Judiciary Committee's Subcommittee to Investigate Juvenile Delinquency, Indiana Senator Birch Bayh voiced his concern this way: "The system's impact on the lives of troubled girls is especially serious, and while it's not surprising that many of the prejudices our society has against females are reflected in the juvenile justice system, the ramifications of such discrimination are shocking."

According to a University of Michigan study, girls receive harsher treatment than boys do for lesser offenses and are kept in detention longer. In a study conducted by the *Yale Law Journal*, New York juvenile court intake officers said that a parent's objection to a daughter's boyfriend would get her into hot water faster than a charge of larceny for a boy. A girl's verbal abuse of her parents was more likely to find her standing in front of a judge than was a boy's physical assault on another person. And a girl who comes home late was more likely to be detained than a boy who was suspected of illegal entry.

"The brutal truth," says John Rector, "is that the young woman who has done nothing more threatening to the state than run away from home is likely to be treated as harshly as a young man who has held up a store."

Judge Lisa Richette, of the Philadelphia Court of Common Pleas, agrees. "Show me a boy brought to detention for promiscuity. You can't. We have a system that is offended only by the sexuality and independence of young women. The courts are acting as legal chastity belts around the waists of young women."

So while girls do have more social freedom than ever before to have sex or to make certain other life-style choices, they don't have nearly as much as we like to tell them they do. But, more important, they are still unable to identify the nature of genuine freedom. So they will "act" free — have sex or drink or stay out late — not out of a sense of real independence, but because that is what boys do and because they are lonely and adrift.

"It is easiest to imitate the most extreme behavior," says Marty Wasserman, chief clinical psychologist in the adolescent medicine division at Children's Hospital of Los Angeles. "What we are seeing is a rebellion from the limiting female role rather than a positive identification with the strong person of either sex who is unafraid of his or her 'feminine' qualities like warmth, gentleness, and openness."

In sum, our young women are finding themselves in a hazardous situation. They hear that almost any kind of behavior is normal (although, again, they are still much more likely than their brothers to be punished if they push the promise too far), but many of us are unable to help them discern what it means to be fully human, so that whatever life-style they choose expresses and enriches their own humanity.

We need to learn more about genuine freedom if we want to help our daughters as well as ourselves to become truly free. We can begin by looking at our ideas about the nature of freedom, about our own strengths and weaknesses and hopes and dreams, and ask ourselves some questions. And then encourage our daughters to ask themselves the same questions.

What is really important to me? What am I trying to prove in the world, and to whom? Do I really need what I think I want? Will what I am after bring me peace, satisfaction, gratitude, and aliveness — or will it merely make me hungrier, more ambitious for more, bigger, and better experiences?

A Stanford professor finds it "ironic and distressing, but not unexpected" that women are paying such a high price for the improvement of their status. All such social victories, he reminds us, have historically extracted a number of sacrifices on all sides.

But I have to take the position that the victories won by these younger women need not include such extreme forms of sacrifice — the suicides and depression, pregnancies that inevitably end in the curtailment of dreams, drug and alcohol abuse, and more.

Such problems may seem to be inevitable in a time when growing up female is a whole new enterprise. But those problems are not *necessary*. I hope that may become clearer throughout this book.

To take license from Mr. Dickens: these are neither the best of times, nor the worst of times. Perhaps for young women they can turn out to be the most promising of times.

# 2

## *Two Different Worlds*

• "MY MOTHER TAUGHT ME never to let men know how smart I was. When I was nineteen and a junior in college — and my mother was never sure why I was in college at all — I applied to medical school. Everyone, including me, was astounded when I was accepted. Mama was outraged. 'Who will marry you if you're a doctor? If you have to *be* anything, then be a teacher.' She died soon after that, and I always took her advice as a sort of deathbed ultimatum. I became a teacher, and while I like what I do, I have always regretted passing up that chance. Consequently, I don't put any limits on my daughter."

• "My daughter is growing up in a safer neighborhood than I did. We live in a comfortable house in a nice, quiet suburb. I grew up in a crowded noisy neighborhood of a big city. Still, I don't think the *world* she is growing up in is as safe as the one I came through."

• "Times may not have changed all that much after all, because Luisa is just as self-conscious about having small breasts as I was when I was her age. The only difference is that I wore padded bras, and she doesn't wear a bra at all. In our own ways, both of us have the same concerns about looking sexy and attracting male attention."

To begin to have any understanding of our daughters, there are two simple things we need to know. The first is that the basic issues all of us must confront in our lifetimes are the same. Questions like "Who am I?" and "What is the meaning of my being here?" bear no relation to time or place or feminism or, for that matter, any other "ism." You are asking those questions. So is your daughter. That has not changed.

The second is that the world, the background, in which she is being asked to come to terms with herself *is* very different from and much more complex than the world in which you grew up. And not merely in terms of woman's place in it, as I have already pointed out.

In this chapter, I will look at how the world has changed since you were your daughter's age, and, given the fact of those changes, what your daughter is finding important enough to believe in and to work toward.

Chances are you lived through World War II, which, though it imposed a good deal of hardship on the homefront population, also served to mobilize our positive and loving qualities. As a people we pulled together and were happy to make sacrifices for the common good.

Then came the fifties, in which home and hearth and the ethic of the nuclear family were all, where television and other outside intrusions on how we lived and how we thought were only beginning to make themselves felt. Families, for instance, still spent evenings talking to one another. It was also the era of the cold war and national chauvinism and the belief that hard work and a college education could open any door.

That is not the way of the world in the 1980s. The rate of change and the number of new pressures is staggering, which in some respects means that this generation has little in common with previous generations.

Before I look at *what* these other new pressures are, I want to back up a step and simply point out *how* much more difficult it is to find your head when so many around you seem to be losing theirs.

Erik Erikson, the developmental psychologist, has postulated that one of the most important tasks of adolescence is the observance of what he calls the "psychosocial moratorium — a period of experimentation with new values, roles, and systems of belief, a "time out" before a young person settles on a more solid identity. The moratorium of adolescence allows a delay of adult commitments and choices that may well set the pattern for the rest of her life.

"The moratorium," Erikson has said, "may be a time for horse stealing and vision quests, a time for Wanderschaft or work 'out West,' a time for 'lost youth' or academic life, a time for self-sacrifice or for pranks."

However Erikson saw this time of "instability" as set against the background of a stable culture that stood ready to welcome the newcomer to the adult fold when she was ready.

But today's adolescent is working out against a much different sort of background the questions of who she is and who she will become. Many of the adults she observes have no more come to terms or found peace with themselves than she has. Many of them are also on extended sexual quests, and many of them are also wondering what they will be if *they* ever grow up.

No small percentage of us adults have become irreligious, untrusting, cynical, even thinking of religion as something to acquire, something we take care of on Sundays or when we are in crisis.

We have grave doubts (if we think about it at all) about the existence of such qualities as truth, beauty, goodness, or harmony. Instead of seeing the truth, we make a big to-do about "letting it all hang out" or "telling it like it is." But wanting to keep what we like to think of as peace in our homes, many of us go to great lengths to avoid confrontation so that real, loving communication gets buried.

Instead of being interested in beholding beauty, we want to be attractive. Instead of recognizing goodness, we want to *feel* good all the time.

As the pop song goes, we are living life in the fast lane, and as Dr. John Bolf, psychologist and director of an adolescent drug abuse program, told me: "As a people, we seem to be living from one crisis to the next, with nothing solid to hang on to in between."

And, in fact, there is a fear that the next crisis will be our last. After all, terrorists boast they have all the ingredients they need to manufacture the bomb that can erase us all. We coexist with the reality of overpopulation, with pollution of the land, air, and sea, and extinction of whole species of plant and animal life. We are so threatened by reports of dwindling supplies of natural resources that we panic when newspapers report a shortage of gasoline or toilet paper.

The result of our fear that tomorrow may be worse or may not happen at all is a virtual obsession with living life to the hilt now, and damn those questionable tomorrows. (This is not at all the same as the Eastern, Zen-oriented view of life that says that time itself is only a conceptual prison that man has invented for his own pain and amusement, and that in spiritual reality — the *only* reality — what man *does* in one minute or in another is of no consequence. By sharp contrast, here in the West, we see time as very real and very serious, and we are forever aware of the seconds ticking away. So we are more and more engaged in the idea to *do* it now, while we still *have* time — as if time were real and belonged to us.)

Often this vain philosophy results in spending too much time and energy trying to keep up with the overachievers next door and a step or two ahead of our creditors. Too often, our relationships with our children suffer.

"In this last generation, there has been a definite weakening of family standards and parental authority," says Dr. Joseph Teicher, director of child and adolescent psychiatry at the Los Angeles County–University of Southern California Medical Center. "There is an increasing number of divorces. And whether or not divorce is part of the picture, more and more children are physically or emotionally abandoned at an early age by parents who are so involved in their own concerns or so troubled and confused, they are not able to give that vital life fluid we call nurturance."

"We have such tremendous need for self-gratification now," says clinical psychologist Vivian Kaplan. "We believe we should only have to do things which make us *feel* good. Grab the gusto while you can because tomorrow may not come at all.

"Few of us are still asking questions like 'What can I leave behind me that will make life better for my children and their children?'"

As a consequence of our emotional shortsightedness, say the experts, our children are growing up without a real sense of purpose or connection to the past or to the future. And a sense of a self not necessarily remembered but accepted as once existing is a guard against despair.

While it is the normal tendency of adolescence to neglect looking to the past as a reminder of better times that were or to the future as a harbinger of better times to come, now the social environment itself supports the idea that today is everything. We no longer hold the attitude that says, "Times may be rough now, but if we existed in the past and we were happy and loved then, it is possible that a joyful, lovable self could also be waiting for us in the future." We simply don't believe that. So we try to get what we can, while we still can.

And if that means we will even compete with our own children to get what we think we need, so be it, as a number of professionals have pointed out to me is happening. Among them, Karen Speros, a high school teacher and counselor who says that "me-itis" has reached epidemic proportions.

"I see so many parents who don't know how to share caring with their kids. Some are even hesitant to share their material goodies. They leave their kids home when they go on trips, and they don't let them drive the family car because they say they don't want to spoil them. At least for some parents, I think it's because they feel it is unfair that their kids get easily the things that came so hard for them."

Other experts have pointed out that while almost all parents truly love their own children, there is a certain national dislike for the idea of teenagers as a group. And all the evidence seems to show that they do weigh heavily on our collective consciousness. Long gone are those lovable scamps like Corliss Archer and Andy Hardy. In their place is the new adolescent stock character in the American bag of stereotypes: irresponsible, self-involved, hedonistic, and absolutely teeming with problems that emerge regularly as horrifying statistics.

Says one young woman, reflecting the thoughts of many others: "There is nothing people my age can do that matters at all to most adults in this country — they don't have the time or the place for or the interest in people who are neither little kids nor adults. We're a waste to them, that's all. They don't like us."

If that, indeed, is how we see our young people, that *is* the way they will see themselves, and the prophecy will continue to fulfill itself. Or as one sociologist archly puts it: society gets the type of adolescent it expects and deserves.

Therein lies another one of those mixed messages that create so much confusion, for while we may not like our teenagers much, on the other hand, we envy them a great deal. Why? Because they have lots of what we think is important in life — youth, unlimited sexual experiences ahead of them, the promise of a future, in general.

So we emulate them. We dress and talk like them, dance their dances, smoke dope, and even try to think like them. We focus on them too much to define our culture. And because we model ourselves after them, rather than pursuing our own values, they respect us less. And it must make them afraid, for if we try to follow along in their footsteps, where is there for them to go? Who will lead them?

And what can young women believe in? In such a world, what are their goals? What do they value? What matters to them? And, what doesn't?

They are unsure of which set of rules to play by, or even whether they have much chance of winning, whichever rules they choose. Perhaps that explains why their interest in feminism as a set of principles or as a course of action is a distant and objective one, at best. For while most believe in concepts like the passage of the Equal Rights Amendment, few are actively involved in the movement, nor do they express more than a passing curiosity in the philosophy of feminism.

According to Elizabeth Jerome, director of the teenage division of the Children's Health Center and Hospital in Minneapolis: "Adolescent girls think feminism is something for ranting and raving older women. It just is not something they see themselves needing now."

One illustration of Jerome's contention that teenage girls take the benefits of the women's movement for granted: a high school in a liberal community in California has tried to offer classes in women's studies every semester for the past few years, but ends up canceling them for lack of student interest.

Neither are girls yet setting their educational or career goals as high as do their male peers. For instance, any number of studies will tell us that girls themselves don't think college is as important for females as it is for males. Often, when they do, according to Jane Gaskell, who in a 1978 study interviewed girls in a Boston high school, they cited reasons like:

• "A guy has to go to college to get a good job and support a family, and to find out about life. A girl has to have something in common with a guy in order to talk to him."

• "You can never tell if you will have to support your family if your husband gets sick."

When it comes to careers, a 1977 Gallup Youth Survey found that girls still look toward traditional female fields, with their top three career choices, in order, being secretary, teacher, and nurse, while boys chose, in order, "skilled worker" (which, though by definition "only" blue collar, includes the enviably lucrative fields of mechanic, carpenter, plumber, and electrician) and engineer and lawyer.

Gertrude Berger, a Brooklyn College professor of education, found that, even among the supposedly more liberal children of professionals, young men still opt for work with fringe benefits like power, profit, leadership, and independence, while girls still home in toward the traditional "female-intensive" fields that offer "interesting experience" as their prime rewards.

Why are the aspirations of young women still lagging so far behind those of their male peers? For starters, the reality is, as I mentioned earlier, that many of the opportunities themselves are still to be found on paper only. Aspirations can be expected to rise substantially only after there is a general upgrading in the social and economic supports for women.

In addition, young women are still expected to have a persuasively good reason for wanting to have careers of their own, and they still hear the implicit — at least — warning not to allow their personal or career goals to get in the way of their femininity. By its very definition, success for a woman is still a much more complicated animal than it is for a man. We not only check to see whether she is good at whatever job she has set out to do, but then we look more closely still to determine whether she is also good at being a *woman* — feminine and sexy, not to mention being a supportive wife and mommy who keeps the home fires stoked. Oh, yes — she must also be very careful not to bruise any male egos on her way up.

So, allowing that those rules are pretty forbidding, we see that girls are not necessarily continuing to choose careers in social service–related areas merely out of a sense of lofty idealism, but because such fields are "safe," sort of halfway stations between home and competition in the high-powered "male" fields. It seems that even today young women about to go to college or choose a career are still highly susceptible to the social disease first described as "fear of success" about fifteen years ago by Matina Horner, psychologist and president of Radcliffe College.

The fear-of-success syndrome is characterized by cold feet brought on by anticipation of numerous dire consequences including loneliness, unpopularity (the extreme result being ineligibility as a marriage partner), and loss of femininity if the "victim" succeeds in "male-identified" fields of endeavor.

Related studies have shown that while girls feel free to compete with boys through the elementary grades, as social acceptance — particularly from the opposite sex — becomes more and more important to them, they become progressively more anxious until their abilities are no longer reflected in their achievements. For the most part, the syndrome doesn't appear when women compete against other women. And, says Horner, the more capable the female, the more she is prone to fear exercising her capabilities.

While males are not immune to the fear-of-success sickness, most of them do learn, practically from Day One, that the consequences of success will be entirely positive. *And*, if they should be afraid, they are taught to face their fears head-on. The importance of such courage has not been emphasized nearly hard enough for the majority of our female children.

The way to cure women effectively of this primarily female malady involves more than telling them they are liberated or establishing a few affirmative action programs. We need to change the way we view men and women and freedom. As clinical psychologist Dione Sommers says: "I see many young women blowing their grades, betraying their strengths. The culture may finally be telling them to 'go for it,' but I don't think it is speaking very loudly, because a lot of young women don't seem to be hearing."

We need to remember that not only does society lose a valuable human and economic asset every time a woman gives up in the name of "femininity," but that the individual who adjusts her sights downward pays an incalculably high price — in frustration, depression, hostility, aggression, bitterness, and confusion.

But things may already be looking up in the female aspirations department. According to teacher and therapist Fern Rubin, girls are becoming more interested in challenging careers, and even more important, she says she sees them becoming more interested in challenging their intelligence.

Another encouraging sign is a 1978 survey of New York City teenagers (admittedly in a more liberal enclave than most areas of the country), which asked boys and girls to indicate their top priorities in life. Both sexes listed "getting a job I enjoy," "preparing for my future," and "making it on my own," as their number one, two, and three goals. For girls, the traditional choices "having children some day" and "getting married" ranked, respectively, at numbers 10 and 14. (The apparent reversal of those two life steps was an interesting finding in itself.)

What else is important — or not — to these young women? Though afraid that the price of success is too high, they are materialistic, but without real conviction that there is any value in being so. For they have seen that the frantic striving to acquire things and people has not worked for their parents, and deep down, they know there is no good reason it should work any better for them, which does not mean they don't still hunger for the Porsche or the $50,000-a-year job.

They have no more faith in the honesty and integrity of the institutions of government and the individuals involved in it than did the kids who grew up in the turbulent late sixties and early seventies but, unlike their older brothers and sisters, they are not outraged by the lack of morality. Rather, they have come to accept it as the status quo.

"Government is crooked, and so are the courts" was a typical comment I heard. "There is no justice when a person carrying an ounce of marijuana can get twenty years and Manson, with all his murders, has a chance to come up for parole."

Says another young woman with a wry smile and a shrug of her shoulders, "We have some wimpy guy for a President who sounds like a bad joke on *Saturday Night Live.* But that's just the way it is, isn't it?"

Shari Glucoft-Wong is a therapist in Berkeley, California, and in a few short years she has seen a remarkable transformation in the political and social climate of an area noted for its extreme youth activism.

"A few years back young people were more interested in the world around them," she says. "They worked against the war and for the environment and civil rights. Now it is more difficult to interest kids in causes outside of themselves because they are busy traveling inward. Sometimes this journey is very narcissistic, but often there is an honest interest in finding out who they *really* are."

And still there are the young women who long for a cause in which to believe and for which to fight. "If there was a Vietnam War to protest against, I would," said a wistful-sounding fifteen-year-old. "I would march and go to sit-ins. My big brother told me all about them.

"The people in the sixties had something to stand up for. We don't have anything like that these days."

What they do have is each other, and so they still believe in man-woman relationships. Yet they are skeptical that those relationships can be happily everlasting. The institution of marriage does not teem with promise for them because they haven't seen a surplus of marriages that impressed them as whole and loving.

"I'm not really thinking about getting married," says a girl who has been through three of her mother's marriages. "I'm too independent. I *would* consider living with a guy as a roommate, you know, platonically, because it is a nice, safe feeling to have a male figure around.

"If I ever did get married, it wouldn't be until I was thirty-five or so. By then I would be mature enough to make sure I would be a hundred percent happy. And then, it would have to be a really equal thing. I can't see myself ever being a typical housewife."

And yet once committed to marriage, this generation apparently does not believe in taking the easy way out if things get a little bumpy. In a 1978 Gallup Youth Survey, teenagers, by a two-to-one margin, said they thought that divorce was too easy to obtain in this country, and that those who do dissolve their marriages have often not tried hard enough to save them.

According to these kids, the two biggest reasons why adults get divorced is that they marry too young and they just can't get along with each other. They also listed money problems, alcohol abuse, and infidelity as contributing factors to the high rate of marital crackups.

Teenagers today are looking for values that can have real meaning for them, values that are bigger than they are, more lasting than the fads with which they have short, passionate flings. They want to believe, to have faith. They want to have the hope, the firm ideals, and the sense of a job well done that they see lacking in the world around them.

We keep offering them what we believe are more and more liberties, but what they want — what we all want — is to *know* who they are and where they belong, and what is right and wrong for them.

And that is how God and the search for an ultimate belief system comes into an individual's awareness. Adolescence, because it is, by its very nature, a time of searching for identity and a place in society and in the universe, is also a time when individuals are ripe for "conversion" — either toward or away from the church, either toward or away from a spiritual orientation toward life. Indeed, the very question most typical of adolescence — "Who am I?" — if not answered too easily or too early, is in itself a spiritual one.

I found, as the experts I interviewed seem to have found, three basic positions on God and religion among young people: the skeptical, the all-embracing, and the open-minded seeking.

In a society where humanistic disciplines emphasize the worship of the God "Me," where "making it under one's own steam" is a highly prized value, and where grinning, flag-waving television evangelists make it appear as if God is either for the weak or the fanatical, it is no wonder that a good number of adolescents have little use for religion.

The skeptical teenagers are turned off by organized religion because, as they see it, churches don't reach out to people in general, and fail to offer programs or ideas relevant to youth in particular. These disenchanted young people also point out that many who attend church with religious regularity forget to practice during the rest of the week what they profess on Sunday.

- "All my parents' church has is boring sermons, bazaars, and Bingo."
- "The people I see in church live their lives like a parody of the 'ideal' Christian, but they don't have any interest in spiritual understanding."
- "My church doesn't challenge me to ask important questions."

Others eschew religion as a "crutch." "And I don't need any crutches. I have my friends and I have me," says a young woman who may be reluctant to recognize her particular brand of crutch.

A common reflection of our fondness for materialism was this fairly typical comment: "I don't see how anyone believes in God. I like things you can touch and prove exist."

And those who see God as a foul-weather friend only: "I've gone through periods of being pious — going to church and reading the Bible and praying — when I was really down. But I did those things because there was nothing else to turn to, and I was never sure I got any results."

But many other young people, feeling helpless and under stress, are turning to a very fundamental concept of the Deity. These are the all-embracers. Bob Iles believes that the basic, charismatic religions appeal to a lot of young people because they are assured of total love and support by God the Christ, and by other church members. They are not asked to *do* anything, to achieve anything for this love. That is a tremendous relief to young people who are weary of trying to prove themselves in a world in which they often feel their efforts are not sufficiently rewarded. Here, the rewards are not only great; they are explicit and everlasting.

Many other young women today are turning away from "old-fashioned" notions like "Everything in the Bible must be accepted at face value," or "God will punish you if you have sex before marriage." For them, God has undergone a metamorphosis from personal friend and mentor with whom bargains can be struck ("Please let Ted call me, and I promise I will study harder") to a power or a life spirit that works for the Good. (The "Force" in the *Star Wars* films is a God concept that quickly caught the fancy of teenagers everywhere. It is an Eastern-oriented idea that says that the power, the love, the intelligence of God is within us all.)

"I don't believe in the traditional God, but I have always felt like I had a God-something inside of me," said a slightly chubby, sweet-faced girl.

Those young women who had at least the beginnings of a set of spiritual values seemed to be less confused about their lives, more confident that, no matter how unordered their adolescence seemed to be, there was another order they could count on.

And these are the young people who are not content to ask "How do I get mine?" but, whether they are aware of it or not, have begun to inquire "What is my task in life? How do I best express myself and make use of the gift of being in the world? How do I love fully?"

These are the questions that have the power to transform their lives.

Many of the young women I spoke to would like to

maintain a spiritual dialogue with their parents, but often find their parents come on as if they were the only ones in the room who could have any answers.

These girls would like to be granted the right to question their parents' beliefs and religious customs, and to look for a more personally relevant concept of God. In time, their faith may appear remarkably similar to that of their parents, but they must make that faith their own, on their own, and from deep within their own convictions.

"My mother's background is much more Jewish than mine. She has all Jewish friends, and dated only Jewish boys as she was growing up. And she has stayed close to the religion. But being Jewish doesn't matter a lot to me right now. I know that bothers my mom, and I'm sorry. I've got to find my own way with God."

So do we all.

# 3

## *Motherly Love and Other Great Expectations*

IF GROWING UP FEMALE is more hazardous than ever before, it follows that the job of mothering the liberated woman-to-be comes complete with its own set of new conditions, pitfalls, and overloaded expectations.

Rest assured; it does. Women are now being asked to raise a new kind of daughter — stronger, more self-sufficient, more resourceful, more determined than ever before — to meet a world in which the terrain is unfamiliar to them. That, in itself, is no easy assignment.

But instead of being patted on the back for trying to do her best in these trying times, Mother tends to catch a lot of anger floating around that says that her best has not been good enough. There is even a whole new literature that ostensibly sheds new light on a neglected area of human relating — mothers and daughters — but that also succeeds at making it legitimate to blame Mother.

These books and films tell us, in glowering black-and-white terms, that Mother is almost single-handedly responsible for her daughter's inability to respond to the delights of liberation. For instance, if your teenager is prone to wandering through the house, Ophelia-like, in a state of chronic melancholia or higher than a kite, get ready to take it on the chin, Mom. If she has the wrong kind of friends, or too few of them, you must be the guilty party. If she chooses a career and puts home and hearth on the back burner until she is thirty, or if she eschews the liberated life and marries a high-school dropout at sixteen, it was probably because you toilet-trained her too early — or too late.

You, Mrs. Portnoy, made her afraid of sex. On the other hand, who else could be responsible for her bedding down with the entire varsity football team?

Mom, it is painfully clear, has been getting a lot of bad press these days. It has become almost de rigueur to rage endlessly at her for her countless flaws. If Freud — or at least the way we have interpreted and misinterpreted him — hadn't done enough to heap guilt and anxiety on mothers, some views of feminism have piled the abuse higher by declaring that motherhood, at best, is an entirely irrelevant way to spend twenty years of one's life.

Therefore, not only it is being suggested that Mother is lurking behind all of those horrific statistics about teenage pregnancy, suicide, drug abuse, and alcoholism, but the whole maternal undertaking was just plain dumb in the first place.

It is almost as if we have come to believe there are three distinct species of people in the world — men, women, and mothers. And women are striving to liberate themselves from the enemy — men and mothers. But mothers are women — ergo, persons — too, and they also deserve to be liberated — liberated from the myths that we still embrace about the condition of motherhood.

Number one is the myth of perfect mother love — a

special quality reputed to come naturally to those who bear children, which rests in a hallowed place above all other forms of human love. While our ideas about this love — that it is omniscient, omnipresent, and infinite — are not new, never before have we been more impressed with it, and never before have we been so quick to be disappointed when Mother doesn't live up to the legend that preceded her.

Part of the myth of motherly love is that it is supposed to protect its progeny from the pains of growing up. (Never mind that no child-care expert has come up with a workable method of raising a child without pain or suffering to all concerned.)

Mother love is supposed to be free of doubt and fear and anger and resentment. Of course, all those things are part and parcel of raising a child. The problem comes in when Mother pretends those things are not there, so her daughter ends up getting unspoken, half-hidden messages (that is, I love you/I love you not all the time, absolutely.) She feels guilty for not appreciating the perfect mother she is supposed to have and Mother feels she has failed to live up to the gospels according to St. Hallmark.

In addition, say psychologists, the daughter who feels cheated because she failed to get the flawless love that was promised is then destined to go through life searching for it, making all of her other intimate and important relationships fruitless attempts to compensate for the lack.

(It is one of nature's more obvious maxims that you cannot recreate that which never existed.)

Today, there is additional anger because Mother and her magic love did not see into the future far enough to prepare her daughter for social, sexual, and psychological liberation. And the literature of liberation often rationalizes — even sanctifies — daughter's anger at her mother's failure to raise her to make it in a world that is very different from the world in which Mother grew up, or even in any world she could possibly anticipate.

"These authors show very little appreciation for their mother's lives, for who they were and what they had to contend with when they were growing up," says psychology professor Judith Stevens-Long. "The motivation behind any of their mothers' behavior seems to be a total mystery to them."

It is important for mothers to remember — and perhaps to remind their daughters — that all of us are the product of our time, of our culture. And because times, especially for women, have changed so drastically in the last generation, it is unfair to ask older women to pay the bill for learning and then teaching their daughters what may now be an obsolete cultural message.

It would also do us good to listen to people like psychologist Stevens-Long when she tells us: "Mother love does not exist separately from all other forms of loving. All there can ever be is the feeling and experience that an individual mother has for an individual child. If you take a thousand women, you would find as many ways of loving.

"God does not have a rubber stamp that says, 'This is mother love,' and 'This is not.' It is to no one's advantage to pretend that mothers have a special ability to love."

For those of us, mothers and daughters, who want to transcend what was, these critics stop far short of the place where growth and renewal become possible. They do no good when they smugly inform Mother her best just doesn't cut it, failing to help her answer questions like "*Where* did I go wrong? How did I disappoint this kid? And is there anything I can do about it now?"

When we conspire to keep intact this myth we become isolated from who we are and from who the other in the relationship is. If we are afraid of making a mistake and mussing up our image, we will keep ourselves from moving in any direction and be unable to respond to what is needed from moment to moment. And trying to be a perfect mother keeps us from getting our own needs met.

As one mother says: "I wish Karen wouldn't always see me as perfect, and all-knowing, and able to do everything. Sometimes *I* need to be dependent and get some mothering. I find myself looking forward to the times she isn't around, because then there is no pressure to 'do it right' for her.

"Sometimes I actually begin to believe that I have the power to destroy her life or to make it perfect, and when she hurts, I feel responsible for giving her the answer that will get her out of it. When she was much younger, I *did* seem to have all the answers she needed. Now I don't. I don't even know what all of her questions are."

We need to face the reality that we aren't going to be perfect mothers, and we certainly are not going to raise perfect children. Do you think that you have the power to ensure that your children are going to be the first generation in history to be free of doubts, anxieties, and hang-ups? If so, think again.

Still, it may be a long time before your daughter lets go of her idea that mothers are people who have all the answers. And because adolescence is a time of such intense self-involvement, you may have to wait until she grows up (which could occur at eighteen, but more often takes place around age thirty) before she can see you — the way you act, what you say, the way you think — apart from its effect on her.

In the meantime, how can we most lovingly respond to our daughters' disappointment when we fail to come up perfect every time?

"I find that what is most helpful, both to my daughter and to me, is to stay out of her ideas about blaming me for not being who she wants me to be," says Fern Rubin. "That means not getting angry or feeling guilty or in any way taking it personally. And I need to remember that there is very little I can do about it.

"It also helps me to get a clearer perspective of the real issues with which she is dealing behind the blaming. For instance, if she is feeling unfree, and blames me for her lack of freedom, it is helpful if I can understand what she calls freedom, and then realize that I cannot take real freedom away from her.

"She may be holding on to the idea that people and circumstances control her life, and I'm one of them. School is another; so is money. And as long as she blames me or anything else, she isn't ready to be free, to be her own person. At best, all she gets is to be an expert on how her problems got to be her problems.

"I am not ignoring her complaint, but if I can see what it is really about, that allows her to see it too, and allows her to move past the problem."

It will be also much easier to be supportive and loving — and truly helpful — to your daughter if you don't think you are obligated, as some mythical matriarchal figure, to have all the answers.

Indeed, that maternal obligation can be stifling. Says one mother with sadness: "It seems I can be a better mother to the kids I work with at the hospital where I am a nurse than I can be to my own daughter. To them, I am everything I ever wanted to be with Cherrie. It must be because no one has any expectations about the way it should be. So everything is a gift."

Another mother, with the perception and patience born of much self-examination, says she has come to understand her daughter's anger and disillusionment with her — although the understanding does not always mean it is much easier to live with. She realized that she had had very similar feelings toward her own mother — feelings she never fully understood until a few years after her mother died.

"I see now that, when I was little, my mother and I both assumed that when I hurt she would always be able to make me feel 'all better.' That worked for years. But then came the point when she no longer had that power.

"My adolescence was really painful. I felt ugly, and no matter how often my mother tried to comfort me, it didn't help. For the first time in my life, there was nothing she could do or say that would make my pain go away. I felt betrayed. My buffer against the big, bad world had deserted me. I blamed her.

"Now I see my rationale in blaming her had been 'Since you are my model in life, and I am to identify with you, then it must be your fault that I suffer.'

"I think Cathy is going through the same stage right now. She is very uncertain of herself and, in some ways, feels I've failed her. We've talked about this, and on an intellectual level she knows I'm not responsible. I think it will take time before emotionally she can surrender the expectation that my love should make everything all right."

We can try to help our daughters see that if they feel we didn't give them everything they need to be all they want to be — constant affection or financial security or a mother who excelled at math or tennis or cookie-baking — they may have to find those things someplace else, instead of being consumed with anger that they didn't get it all precisely where they think they should have. That expectation, after all, is just part of the myth.

The insistence on the inviolability of mother love is only one example of the great expectations that mother and daughter reserve especially for the other. And, if anything, our ideas about what liberation is supposed to do for us have only fueled those expectations.

"Daughters are telling their mothers, in so many ways, 'Be a Supermom,' " says Berkeley therapist Edith Kasin. " 'Be home when I'm there — especially when I'm hurting. Keep the house clean and me well fed. On the other hand, accomplish something for yourself. Get a degree or find a job so I don't have to be successful for both of us nor be ashamed of you.'

"For their part, mothers say to daughters, 'Be a Superkid. Get A's, be pretty, sexy, loving, and strive for something important in life. Find strength and independence, the right man and a good match — yet don't leave me far behind.' "

Despite the fact that the women's movement is now pointing out that there are other ways of finding fulfillment than investing everything in home and family, it appears that the message has come a little late for many of the women who are now mothers of teenagers. Since our youth-worshipping society still tends to devalue women as they get older, it is no wonder that many middle-aged or soon-to-be-middle-aged women think the only way they can get any of the goodies is through their daughters. They are another chance to "do" life right, to achieve what the older women can never hope to achieve for themselves.

Simone de Beauvoir has pointed out that many a woman "hopes to compensate for her inferiority by making a superior creature out of one whom she regards as her double; and she also tends to inflict on her the disadvantages which she has suffered. Sometimes she tries to impose on the child exactly the same fate. . . . Sometimes, on the contrary, she grimly forbids the child to resemble her. She wants her experience to be of some use. It is one way of having a second chance."

It is tragic that so many women have gotten the message that, because they have not had exciting careers, nor in some other way made themselves heard in the world, they have failed at life.

Some women, as de Beauvoir has said, are thus asking their daughters "to compensate for their imagined inferiority" by trying to sell them a fine bill of shoulds. Some current favorites: she should be married to a man who won't hurt her. She shouldn't be dependent on a man. She should have a better marriage, and if that doesn't work, a better divorce than I did. She shouldn't be afraid to make it on her own. She shouldn't have any sexual problems — as I did. But, while she should feel freer sexually, she should be careful not to get pregnant at fifteen. With all the opportunities she has laid out in front of her, she should have a better life than I did. (Go out and win one for Ma.)

Annemarie, sixteen, is an open-faced girl with curly red hair and brilliant green eyes. Her father is an accountant. Her mother is a housewife who will always feel self-conscious about the undeniability of that fact. She wants to make sure Annemarie makes no such mistake.

Annemarie is uncomfortable with the expectations her mother and society have for her. "There is pressure on us to break into new fields," she says with a tired shrug. "A lot of us would be content to do something that our mothers did. But we don't want to sound ridiculous saying, 'My goal is to be a housewife.' "

But even women who themselves have been successful outside the home are not exempt from the temptation to push their daughters to make it at least as big as they did.

Explains one young woman, who is in the middle of her senior year in high school: "I feel enormous pressure from my mother, who is a lawyer, to go to college and have an important career. She *says* that that isn't true, and yet I know she would feel as if she failed me if I didn't do as well as she has done in life."

Those sorts of great expectations can be very damaging. "Especially now, with the opportunities newly available to women, mothers are giving their daughters the message: 'Be better than me,' " says therapist Sherry Mandan. "That is a devastating message, and a tremendous burden to live up to. The daughter may try, but she may also constantly worry that someone will find out she is a fraud and a failure. She feels as if she is in borrowed clothes and that it is only a matter of time until the jig is up."

Essie Lee, a professor at Hunter College, also believes that when a parent expects her daughter to achieve for her — manipulating, demanding, and overindulging her to gain that end — the girl can be so stifled with anxiety that she won't be able to experience life on her own terms, as a functioning, independent woman.

Some girls, it has been suggested, are becoming pregnant or dropping out through liquor or drugs or deep depressions as a way of putting down a foot and warning, "Don't count on me."

"My mother always told me she wants me to have things

better than she did," says Alison. "She tells me I'm prettier, so I should have more dates than she had. She tells me I have to get a better education so I can be smarter and have more money. Then I won't have to depend on men the way she has always had to.

"I really do appreciate her wanting me to have things better, but sometimes I can't help thinking I'm not good enough for her just the way I am."

Other girls echo Alison's sentiments:

• "She says it doesn't matter, but I still *feel* this pressure to go to college and have a career before I get married. Because she did the opposite, and now she's sorry."

• "I see a lot of my friends' mothers pushing them to do the lawyer routine. They want them to be the things they didn't have the opportunities to be. A lot of them did the housewife number their whole lives and now they regret it. But that really shouldn't have anything to do with us."

• "Sometimes I really think that my mother is waiting for me to make her happy. And that really scares me."

If your message to your daughter is "Who I am is unimportant, and what I have accomplished is of no value," then even your most minimal expectations for her can be overwhelming because you are, in essence, saying, "I want it to be better for you, but I don't have the slightest idea or hope of how that can happen."

It is important that you learn to acknowledge the value of your own life. While you may not be able to do that in terms of years of higher education or glamour jobs or exciting travel, you can begin to find worth in *who* you are. And it is important to become clear about the difference between what you want for your daughter and what she needs for herself.

"It isn't easy to separate your own confusion and needs

from that of your daughter," admits Fern Rubin, a therapist and the mother of two teenage girls. "If I am honest, when I look at my daughters, I often see my own thoughts, my own need to make things work in a certain manner — even though 'things' are probably working just the way they should.

"As parents, we try to will our children's lives to be a prescribed way, what we think would be best for them and for ourselves. But I think the essential purpose of having children is to challenge that idea and to come to accept what the child is herself and how *life* directs her.

"There is far more beauty in the way things really are than most of us are capable of understanding, so we keep trying to make it better. Our inability to see how exquisitely better it *already is* keeps us trying to make it the way we want, the way we think it should be. That is far more limiting."

Therefore, if you succeed in making your daughter into what you think she ought to be, you will undoubtedly end up limiting her tremendously, because you can't begin to fathom her potential. You can only influence it to come out in a way that *feels* right and comfortable for you — which is far less than the natural beauty and intelligence of her own response to life.

"I see a lot of parents who wear the crowns of their kids' achievements as though they have earned them," says one mother. "That is just so much bull. What Jan does is really no reflection on me.

"I tell her, 'Whatever you do with your life is OK. I'll look at the options with you, but all the decisions are yours, kid. Don't you dare choose a college in town just because it's close to Mama. Go there if you think you'll get the best education. If you think you'll get the best on the other side of the country, go there. If you don't want to go to college, don't. If you want to work in a bakery, do it.' "

Anger, blaming, guilt, and preoccupation with thwarted expectations allow us only to look backward, never ahead. They catch us up in the past, not letting us take a real step into the future to genuine liberation.

So, growing up — hers and ours — means separating our expectations from hers. We need to be more interested in what is truly her way of expressing life and less interested in what we want for her.

But don't browbeat yourself if that interest isn't easy for you, for when your daughter reaches adolescence, it is natural to begin to identify with her more strongly than ever, and she with you. And liberation has only made the process of seeing where you end and she begins much more complex — and interesting, as we shall see in the next chapter.

# 4

## *Mirror, Mirror on the Wall*

• "I HAVE A SON and a daughter. I love them both equally. But there is something very different in my relationship with my daughter. I understand her better because I've already gone through what she is going through now.

"The things she is experiencing now — her first period, her first date, her first formal — I remember. Watching her — even though I know times today are very different — is like watching a replay of myself."

• "Until I was thirteen, my mother dressed us in matching outfits. Finally, I told her I needed to dress like myself — though at the time, I didn't have any idea who that was. I'm seventeen, and she still identifies with me completely. She's always surprised to find that my opinions on a lot of things are different from hers, and that my best subjects are math and science, when hers were drama and music. I know she wanted me to do something like go into the theater, but that's just not me.

"I wonder how old I'll have to be before she gives up trying to shape me into her idea of what her daughter should be."

• "I see the relationship I have with my mother as more important than any relationship I will ever have with a man," says a very new woman. "My mother will be with me forever — a part of me — and I don't necessarily see the man-woman relationship like that."

Adolescence is the time of our lives when we strain to see who we are, and who and what we wish to become. "Identity formation," as the experts tell us, is one of the major psychological tasks we seek to accomplish before we exit from adolescence. And while the resolution of a young girl's identity has certainly never been a separate matter from her relationship with her mother, the changing place of women in the world today has linked the two issues with even more certainty.

Your daughter has identified and does identify and, to some extent, will always identify with you. There is no way either of you can get away from the irrevocability of that simple fact of nature. For it was from you she first learned the meaning of being a human being. It was in your body that she glimpsed the possibilities of femaleness and femininity, although she may very well be a teenager before the psychic resemblance shows itself.

"When girls are very young, even though both mother and daughter are members of a common gender, their lives take place in such different realms, with such different interests, that there does not appear to be all that much identification going on," says therapist Shari Glucoft-Wong. "But teenage girls become very tuned in to their mother's self-image, because their lives start looking more and more similar — particularly in the case of a single mother who may also be dating, or a mother who is going back to school or who is resuming a career. Who you are, what you think about, and what you do become much more important to her."

It is not surprising that many mothers whose careers have been concentrated in the home are now concerned that who they have been and what they have done are not adequate as role models in a world that is asking more of their daughters than it did of them. And they are afraid that the messages they gave them were needlessly limiting.

In essence, they are afraid for their daughters to identify with them.

"How do I reverse what I taught her when she was a little girl?" asks a woman who became a midlife feminist. "I only told her what I thought was important then, you know, the whole 'happily ever after' story. I think that I am a stronger, more independent person now, but I'm still afraid she may think she has to wait until midlife to be a complete, expressive human being."

But in these days when liberation is often a compulsive clarion call, you needn't disqualify yourself as a model for your daughter simply because you haven't garnered laurels outside the home. All that time, when Madison Avenue thought your prime interest was watching the clothes go round and round in the washing machine, it is very likely that you were also concerned with less mundane matters, thank you.

"I have found that during all of these housekeeping and child-rearing years, most women do a lot of pondering and thinking about important issues," points out Peggy Golden, "whereas oftentimes their husbands were so busy trying to shoot up the ladder of material success that they had no time to think about ethical and spiritual matters."

These women can provide very rich models of "being" for their daughters. They need to stop, become aware of what they have to offer, and give themselves credit for that. *Then* they may want to help their daughters take note of other women who do have careers in which their daughters might be interested, and see if it might be helpful for mother, daughter, and these models of other possibilities to sit down together and talk.

Also, the women who put themselves down for their in-house careers should be aware that life is not so simple for the women of their generation who have followed roads with higher prestige. Because, as Shari Glucoft-Wong reports, it is not at all unusual for *their* daughters to feel as if they have been cheated in the mothering department.

"I'm getting more calls than you might think from freaked-out mothers whose kids had just come back from visits to grandmothers, armed with questions like 'Why isn't our house like Grandma's?' 'Why don't you make homemade bread?' and 'Why can't we all have dinner together every night?' " As a result, the mothers of these contentious teenagers are also feeling guilty and torn. They want to know how they can live their own lives and still be the kinds of mothers their daughters apparently feel they should be.

So it is not crucial, after all, for you to go around the house humming, "I am woman, hear me roar," to qualify you as a positive model for your daughter. No matter what accomplishments you have racked up in the worlds of high finance or how many degrees you have tacked on your wall, when it comes to being a model, your ability to love without conditions, to be truly grateful for beauty, to experience joy, to appreciate harmony are far more important. If she learns something of those qualities in your home, she will be blessed. And she can do or be almost anything.

Conscious feminists or staunch traditionalists notwithstanding, as your daughter shows definite promise of growing up and finding womanhood, each of you will find herself, often unconsciously, noticing the many ways you are both alike and different from one another.

• "My mother and I both set a lot of goals and demand a lot of ourselves. We care about others and seem to attract needy people into our lives. In that way, I guess you could say we are both really motherly.

"How are we unlike? She beats around the bush when she has something on her mind. I say, 'C'mon, get to the point.' She lets things stew inside her. I'm too impatient for that."

• "Liza worries more than I do about what others think of her, whether they accept her or not, but maybe that's normal for her age. And she hasn't learned yet that, in this world, you have to make a lot of compromises. She still thinks that compromising means she is selling out."

• "My mom thinks life should be easy. I'm more hardworking and less fancy-free than she is. I have more respect for going to college and having a career."

• "My mother and I are both very intelligent. But she's more analytical, where I'm more emotional. Other differences? I won't get married as early as she did — if I get married at all."

• "Deenie and I are both basically positive, happy people. But she is more judgmental, more likely to see the world in black-and-white terms. And I'm also more outgoing and spontaneous, while she seems content to stay home and read and ponder."

• "Sharon never seemed to have any of the insecurities I had as a child — like I still do. She didn't have to move from place to place like I did, and she never saw her father and me fighting the way I saw my parents constantly go at it.

"I think she is a more stable individual, even though the times are much less stable. But, come to think of it, so far she does seem to pick the same kind of men I lean toward, guys that don't have a very high regard for who we are."

But identification is not always conscious or apparent or deliberate. As one mother says: "It isn't so much that I see her identifying with my personality, but that she has decided to go into the same field I'm in. So I do see her preparing the way to identify her *position* in life as she has seen me identify mine.

"And she is interested in boys who are very much like her father, and that I see as another way of identifying with me — by choosing a man like the one I chose."

(What's that old song? "I want a guy just like the guy who married dear old Mom.")

As a part of the evolving process of establishing her own identity, it is normal, it is natural for her to yearn to be like you in certain ways, to be completely mortified when she is told she resembles you in other ways.

For a while, the more she gains awareness — even subconscious awareness — that she is, indeed, like you, the more she may resent the fact — and you. That's because she wants to think of herself as an individual, different from everyone else — especially from you.

And so she may need to cast you, temporarily, in the role of archantagonist. Therapist Barbara Hayes says that, on some level, all girls ask themselves, "How can I have a relationship with my mother, using her to define what I want to be as well as what I don't want to be?"

And when a young woman does measure herself against

her mother, the first reaction is almost always one of deficit. 'Why didn't you . . . ?' 'Why weren't you . . . ?' This anger is often a necessary step in the separation process (which will be discussed in chapter 13).

While it doesn't entirely negate the sting, realizing that this is a process that young girls commonly go through should help a little. And remember that you probably went through a similar process with your own mother: no matter who your mother was, you had some need to prove that you could do life differently.

You can hear this same need when you ask teenagers how they would raise daughters differently from the way their mothers brought them up.

"I won't be so protective," says a vehement seventeen-year-old. "I'll let her make her own mistakes. If I break my heart over some guy, I learn a lot more than if I stay away from him just because she told me to."

"I don't want to be like my mother," says an absolutely certain sixteen-year-old. "I'd never be as strict with my daughter. I won't worry about her all the time. I won't have to if I've raised her right.

"And I'll have my own life so my kids won't have to be a crutch for me. My sister and I *are* our mother's life since my dad left."

Says a fourteen-year-old: "I know one way I would raise a daughter differently. I would teach her to love herself more. It's funny — or maybe, more like it's sad — there are so many things I can't stand about my mother, and yet her approval is more important to me than anyone else's in the whole world."

In fact, both mothers and daughters are often more critical of the ways they are alike than the ways in which they are different. Few of us, irrespective of age or gender, accept qualities in others that we can't abide in ourselves. And a mother can manage to hide from something she doesn't like in herself until she sees her daughter acting out that quality. For then she must not only face herself, but she must encounter her legacy.

And when a young girl sees a quality in herself that she would rather deny, and perceives the same quality in her mother, she sees her destiny. That can be, at the least, disquieting. She thinks she needs her mother to be someone better to make it possible for her to transcend the parts of her she doesn't like.

"The things I hate about myself are the things that are like my mother," says blonde, moonfaced Annie Crocetti. "She is always upset because she is never on time getting places or doing things. I procrastinate the way she does. Somehow I can never get to school on time.

"And there is something worse. She doesn't think I notice, but she drinks too much. And I have begun drinking a lot more than I should. I wonder if she is aware that I drink, but is afraid to say anything because then I'd confront *her*. Wouldn't it be funny if we started hiding our bottles in the same places around the house?"

"I get really mad when my mother lets men step all over her," says the sixteen-year-old daughter of a divorced mother. "When I have a hard time saying 'no' to the boys I know, I feel like it's because of the example she sets for me."

But it's interesting that a daughter is rarely critical of a not especially admirable quality she shares with her mother, as long as her mother has come to peace with that part of herself. "I may be quick to anger," says a mother, "but that is a part of me. I try to understand it, but I don't put myself down for it. Gerry is the same way. We have some real riproaring arguments, but then we laugh about it. It's no big deal."

Social scientists point out that a young girl often takes on the characteristics she least likes in her mother, because it is less frightening to internalize — to *become* — those qualities and to hate *herself* than it is to hate her mother. We are, most of us, simply afraid of losing our mother's love and respect.

But if we — daughters who are already mothers and daughters who may or may not ever become mothers — are to live full, loving lives, it is essential that we make a place for the mother within us. Especially the parts of her of which we are not particularly proud.

"I am really aware of the parts of me I don't like — like the need to be right all of the time or the way I deny anger," says Fern Rubin. "I see those things in my mother. I see them in me. And now I see them in my daughter.

"But I am learning not to be afraid of those things. It is only when I can accept them that I can begin to have the freedom to change them."

Virginia Satir, the pioneer in family therapy, says: "When I work with families, I try to get them to acknowledge the things they don't like about themselves. You would be surprised how often a parent and a child will agree on the same negative traits. But once we get those things out of the way, the positives, the things they've always admired in themselves and in each other, begin to flow."

For a daughter, one sign of genuine liberation has to include admitting that she does indeed, in a multitude of large and small ways, take after her mother — and that that is not such a bad thing after all. Then she will no longer need to feel guilty for wanting to be different in some ways, or for seeking another sort of life than her mother's because she will realize that her differences do not constitute a rejection of who her mother is.

This identification business, as already implied, goes two ways. Mothers identify with their daughters because daughters are the vessels that carry forth their mythologies, their dreams, their future. Again, that has probably never been more true than it is right now that there are so many more dreams and possibilities that carry the promise of coming true.

"I see Katy as all the things I wanted to be at her age, but wasn't," says Marcy Graham. "She is very outgoing; I was totally introverted. She's popular; I wasn't particularly. She is much more aware of all the possibilities than I was at her age.

"Sometimes though, I have to admit I overidentify with her," her mother says nervously, "so strongly, in fact, that at times she seems to become me and I, her. Her life is *mine.* I don't have that problem with my son because his experiences and perceptions are too different."

Marcy Graham's feelings are not at all uncommon; she just may be more aware of them than other mothers are. But it is that awareness that may help a mother to keep hands off when she wants to mold her daughter's life. As we saw in the last chapter, some women see in their daughters fresh opportunities to become again what they missed out on the first time, another chance to perfect the distortion they see when they look in the mirror.

And these days, when both gray hair and motherhood are not high on the scale of most-admired traits and states of being, it should not be too surprising that many a woman, when staring into that symbolic mirror, has a hard time identifying with the unrelenting reality that she is the mother of a teenager. Instead, she may turn to another sort of identification, one that is not so bruising to the fragile ego. She becomes, as best she can, her daughter's sister. She tells others: "Oh, we are much more like friends than mother and daughter."

While some competition is inevitable between mother and adolescent daughter, in the families where Mom is most interested in being siblings with her daughter, there may often be more rivalry than is healthy.

"I know a lot of girls whose mothers try too hard to be modern or up-to-date on the latest fashions," says a young girl. "They compete for who can look the foxiest and have the most boyfriends. They hang around all the time when their kids' friends come to visit. These girls hate it when their mothers try to be seventeen. What they want and need is a mom."

Instead, what they get is a pal who is often really a rival. Or they get someone who finds it is safer to be a friend than a mother, given our notions about mothers these days.

"I don't feel very comfortable when I'm aware I am 'feeling like a mother,'" admits Fern Rubin. "Our idea of mother is overresponsible, overprotective, and very limited. There are times when I want to see myself as more vital, freer, even more bohemian than the prevalent mother image allows. But I *am* learning to see myself as those things without having to abdicate my motherliness or trying to be my daughters' friend *instead* of their mother."

While being a daughter's friend or peer may seem safer than risking her disapproval, "In the end, you win nothing by trying to be popular with your kids," points out Dr. Gary Strokosh, director of adolescent medicine at Rush-Presbyterian Hospital in Chicago.

"Parents who are interested in scoring points find them-

selves giving in to what they think their kids want to hear.
And they are often wrong. Kids really do look for some
'unpopular' things from you. They want clearly defined
restrictions and a loving, but stronger, hand. They want
good advice, whether or not it is the easiest way.

"I've seen too many of these kids testing their mothers'
'friendship' by pushing them to see if they really care."

A mother who finds herself seeking her daughter's constant approval might find it helpful to talk to her about it.
"Look, the reason I act this way sometimes is because it's
really important to me how you feel about me." That gives
the daughter the opportunity to understand her mother's
behavior and to express love for her, and to tell her what
she really needs from her.

Arlene Epstein is a mother who appears to have her
priorities straight on this matter: "You only get one chance
to be a kid, and a kid needs a mother. She needs her to
point the way, to be a role model, to have more control
over her daughter than her daughter has over her. My
daughter and I talk a lot, and I don't always try to be the
authority. We are associates in life. We talk about feelings
and issues important to both of us. We *share* friendship.
But we are not contemporaries, and at this point in our
lives, there is never any doubt that *I* am the mother. Later
on, we will have a lot of time to be peers."

Some women are frightened by their daughters' apparent differences. Others are proud of them. But women can
be supportive of very different daughters, and they need
to remember that it is all right to come out of different
molds. Liberation — real liberation — includes allowing a
daughter — or a mother — to be different.

"Just because you are my daughter or my mother, I
don't insist you share everything with me," says Virginia

Satir. "I make it possible for you to be selective about the parts of me you want to emulate. And though I am a woman, and you are my daughter, who is becoming a woman, I will remember that we are different people."

And remember, you are not doing your daughter a favor by trying to be more (or less) "liberated" than what is comfortable for you. In time she will come to realize that genuine freedom has much more to do with your acceptance of who (not *what*) you are than it does with whether you carry the banner of a cause, however worthwhile.

We need to be aware that we are lugging around a lot of ideas that we are not yet ready to give up, and that some of us aren't especially comfortable — maybe we never will be — owning a lot of "liberation." And others of us are not comfortable spending the bulk of the day in the home.

"We have to be careful not to develop a new set of myths and clichés about the way it is *supposed* to be, nor should we get caught in a trap that is really no better for us than the old, restrictive notions of the 'good life,' " says Edith Kasin. "We have to learn to respect our own ideas of what works for us, what we know is fitting, ethical, and decent, and respond to life through those."

*That* sort of self-respect makes us, as women, as human beings, as spiritual beings, *worth* identifying with.

And take heart in the knowledge that the closer your daughter comes to having a sense of who she is and what she is about, oftentimes the better your relationship with her can be. At least that was the finding of Dr. Jill Allen, a psychologist at the City University of New York. Not only do girls who have already seen the worst of their identity crises have much more loving and accepting relationships with their mothers, but they also feel more comfortable acknowledging the ways they are like their mothers and more able occasionally to risk being critical of them (and allowing their parents the same privilege) without fear of losing their mothers' love in the bargain.

So, the more either of you can come to realize you are independent, distinct individuals — although cut from the same maker's cloth — the easier it will be to acknowledge and appreciate your samenesses and your differences.

"I look in the mirror now and I see my mother when she was getting old," says Edith Kasin, with a bemused smile. "I look at my daughter, and though I doubt that she can see it yet, I see some of the same things in her. And I wonder if she is going to be able to do it differently, achieve some things I didn't get around to, fulfill herself in ways I wasn't able to or ways that weren't open to me. Will she be able to take pleasure in some of the ways she is like me?

"And how much will she resent me for what I was not able to teach her? How angry will she be when she has trouble doing what came to me so easily? Will she be disdainful of me if she can do easily what was too painful for me to even attempt?"

However uncomfortable you are with who your daughter appears to be at this time in your life, those who work with teenagers and their families, and mothers and daughters who have graduated past the teenage years, promise hope — hope that may very well not manifest itself until the girl is well into or out of those years.

Once she gets past the great biological surgings and has begun to get her own direction and focus, there is very often a reconnecting, a new friendship. It is one that goes beyond "You are my child and you are/are not fulfilling a part of me" or "You are my mother, and therefore should be a certain kind of woman so that I can feel comfortable in my own womanhood."

And there will be wonderful times when you are able to see that the issues she confronts and the joy she experiences *are* yours. *Not* that you are vicariously experiencing those things through her, but that the two of you are seeing with a single eye at the moment, and there is no mother and no daughter, no mature woman and no young girl. Both of you become an awareness of all the possibilities, and for an instant you realize that is all you are. And that is all that matters.

As one mother said: "The moments I feel 'enlightened,' I see her as separate from me, and not even as my child, but as God's child. Of course, there are times when it is necessary for us to play the mother and daughter roles, but the reality is that we are two human beings struggling with living, sometimes more together than at other times."

A wise nineteen-year-old young woman puts it more simply: "I see my mother as a person now. I accept her faults. Now it's OK with me when she cries, when she gets frustrated. I see her hold up under the pressure of her job and of raising a family. I know things haven't been easy for her. I haven't always been easy to live with. I really admire the way she hangs in there when things are bad.

"I see that if she can do it, so can I."

# 5

## *Sex: It's the Same Old Song but Someone Switched the Lyrics*

"THE FIRST TIME I HAD SEX was on my fifteenth birthday," confides Claire, who has yet to see sixteen. "It was supposed to be my big present to myself — my way of saying, 'Now I'm free, and I'm like everyone else.' I guess I'm glad I got it out of the way, but it didn't make me feel any freer. Actually, I felt pretty alone.

"Everybody may be doing it now, but I just don't see what the big deal is."

Claire's wry and jaded observation pretty well sums up the state of the teenage sexual revolution. There are all sorts of statistics that offer solid testimony that while more and more kids are "doing it," few are finding the experience everything their friends or the movies hinted it would be.

Let's see what the statistics have to tell us about sexuality among the very young.

• More teenagers are having intercourse, at an earlier age, and with more partners than at the beginning of the 1970s, according to the Johns Hopkins Schools of Medicine and Public Health.

• More than half of the 21,000,000 teenagers in this country over the age of fifteen, and one of every five thirteen- and fourteen-year-olds, are sexually active. In certain even more precocious areas of the country, the percentage of young people who have had sex is said to be considerably higher.

• And in seeming testimony to the liberation of young females in particular, the Department of Health, Education and Welfare assures us that, in a recent seven-year period, while the rate of premarital intercourse for juvenile men rose by "only" 50 percent, it absolutely soared by 300 percent for females.

Then there are the figures that only begin to give us an inkling of the fallout from the jump in sexual activity:

• More than half of those who have intercourse shun any form of contraception.

• Nearly a third of all sexually active girls will get pregnant before leaving their teen years. That adds up to a million pregnancies every year — or one in every ten girls.

• Girls under twenty account for over 35 percent of all abortions. Another 150,000 a year will have miscarriages; 600,000 will give birth. (In a later chapter, we will consider the physical, mental, and social traumas of pregnancy, childbirth, and motherhood for "women" who are still very nearly children themselves.)

• Among all age groups, fifteen-to-nineteen-year-olds have the second highest rate of venereal disease (12 for every 1,000 individuals). And the incidence of gonorrhea is rising even faster for young females.

However, though numbers may not lie, neither do they convey all of what is really going on here. It is obvious that there has been a coup d'état of sorts in the sexual behavior of this generation of teenagers, but the more things appear to be changing, the more our daughters are finding that becoming sexually active does not lead to instant freedom or even, in many cases, a whole lot of gratification. For these girls who are in such a rush to leave their girlhood behind are now having to face the fact that the emotional and physical consequences of too-early sexual activity are often much more than they bargained for.

In short, most young women are not nearly as free and breezy as the statistics and all the media hype keep going on about.

Neither the statistics nor the uncertainty and confusion behind all those numbers should come as a great shock to us. If our children are more involved in sexual adventuring than we were when puberty struck us, they have grown up in much different times. It is likely that before they entered school they passed a television set and heard terms like "sexual liberation," "open marriage," and "alternative (sexual) life-styles" praised by their proponents and exponents.

But, as in other areas of human intercourse, our messages to our children about sexuality have often not been clear. For instance, even though books like *The Joy of Sex* were a common decoration on many of our coffee tables, it must not have been so difficult for our children to discern that the values around sex which many of us clung to too often had little to do with qualities like joy, harmony, and full expression of self. And while the party line has boasted that women no longer need to be passive captives of the sexual double standard, how often in reality has that meant that female persons now feel just as compelled as males to strut their stuff in bed?

In their lifetimes, teenagers have even witnessed the birth of a profession, that of the sex therapist, created solely to treat our sexual aches and pains. While it is undeniably a positive thing that we are finally dealing with those ills, could it be that the rates of some of those "dysfunctions" have shot up in the last several years concomitantly with our belief that nothing less will do than the multiple orgasms and marathon erections we have been promised by these selfsame sex experts if only we can learn to "do it" right?

Another common sight in our children's formative years has been the legions of individuals in their twenties, thirties, forties, and even beyond who, in their repeated attempts to find the happiness they failed to get in a relationship with that single significant other, have become what we used to call promiscuous.

It is true that teenagers are getting the message that the "older" generation is learning to express, rather than repress, themselves, but how often do they catch us feeling uncomfortable, disappointed, or guilty after the fact? How often would we rather just have sex than talk to those who matter to us, including our children, about what it means?

While in the next chapter I am going to take a closer look at how mothers are reevaluating their own sexuality in the light of their daughters, and how both mothers and daughters are learning to talk to each other about their values and feelings about sex, I think it would be helpful to first take a more holistic view of sexuality, and then to clarify further what sex means to these young women.

What are sex and sexuality, then? While the dictionary tends to offer either definitions structural, functional or reproductive in nature, sex is — or can be — much more. It can be more than sensation-seeking, or a means of testing our attractiveness quotient — both of which are essentially dehumanizing to ourselves and our partners.

Our sexuality gives us the opportunity to explore our

humanity and expose our deepest selves. In the broadest sense, it affects the way we see ourselves and others as male and female — masculine and feminine — persons. As such, it colors all of our experiences, past rememberings, future anticipations. No matter how liberated from sex roles we become, we will always grow up with an awareness of our gender and our sex, though it is up to our parents and the rest of the world what those things will mean to us, whether we will be helped or hindered as we try to find out what we are about. They bequeath us their feelings and fears about sex through their attitudes about elimination, masturbation, and sexual modesty.

All human beings are sexual, and have always been so. Sex is not something that pops up at puberty and dries up and blows away at sixty. Neither is it only a part you play when you slip between the sheets after the lights have been turned off. "When you leave home in the morning, you don't take off your sexuality and leave it on the hall table," says Bob Iles. "Many of us have trouble integrating our sexuality into our total personality. Children are smart enough to know how nice it is to touch. By the time we grow up, we often forget that."

When pontificating to a very young woman about the meaning of sexuality, psychologists sometimes make grand statements like "The first sexual intercourse is one of the most important psychological events in a young girl's life." And the event *can* mark a declaration of independence and autonomy and a quest for acceptance from parents, an affirmation, or at least a questioning, of identity, sexual or other; and a statement that she has enriched her capability to be meaningfully intimate with another.

A young woman brings to the experience her temperament, her ideas about what should be, her attitudes about herself and others, her fears, hopes, memories, her goals. All of these are shaped by the whole of her history, especially that within her family. As she seeks the answers to who she will be, she will try on different kinds of relationships, some of them sexual.

"A girl's sexual expression may be a way for her to tell her parents, 'You don't own my sexuality,' " points out therapist Peggy Golden. "While adults often find adolescent sexual experimentation irresponsible, it can be very responsible from the young person's view. Oh, the time and the place may be totally inappropriate, but it can still turn out to be a loving act of self-validation and assertion."

For some teenagers, sex does mean sharing intimacy, and is faced realistically:

• "I care a lot about David, and making love with him is a natural extension of our feelings, and an important part of our whole relationship."

• "Why shouldn't I make love with someone I care about? Don't tell me to wait until I get married. I don't even know that I will get married. And don't tell me that waiting will make it better. I'm not that unrealistic. It's like my first kiss. Bombs didn't explode. I don't expect sex to be the best thing that ever happened to me, so I don't expect to be disappointed."

• "The whole idea of 'losing' your virginity is so funny. What are you losing? Some girls think of their virginity as a big burden, so they want to lose it as fast as they can. A lot of kids have definite plans to lose it in their senior year. Others say they are going to hold on to it as long as they can. I'm not proud or ashamed that I've been a virgin this long. When the time is right, I'll have sex. And I hope I won't think of it as losing anything."

For countless other young girls, their understanding and

acceptance of themselves as sexual beings, whether or not they are sexually active, is not nearly as sophisticated or all-together as the above comments might indicate. (But, given the nature of the society we have all grown up in, isn't it difficult to expect otherwise?)

While on the one hand, today's youngest women bravely declare their acceptance of sex between consenting adolescents, on the other, most still wonder if it is morally OK to sleep with one boy and go out with others. In the name of liberation, they try not to be jealous if a boy they made love with turns his attention elsewhere. But, try though they might, they can't quite help themselves. While hungry for honest communication, they are embarrassed if a parent wants to talk about sex. ("Aw, Mom, I've heard all that before" is much more likely to reflect discomfort than it is impatience.)

There are differences between us — the other generation — and them, but the differences are often a matter of cosmetics. "Girls today do have access to more information, and there is a greater variety of methods of protection available to them," agrees therapist Maurie Cullen, who teaches classes in teenage sexuality. "They are freer about not wearing a bra and showing their bodies — and they undoubtedly have a larger repertoire of sexual behavior than did most of their mothers.

"But they are not more comfortable. I know one girl, for instance, who claims she has 'laid' sixteen guys, and she sounds as if she's proud of that. But I want to know, why is she keeping tabs? What does that mean? Is this how she is measuring her worth in the world?"

A number of studies have estimated that a large percentage of all sexually active adolescents report guilt and anxiety once the act is accomplished, with the guilt quotient rising even higher among girls.

Apparently, many girls are "comfortable" enough to engage in the act of sex, but not so comfortable to ask the boy to wear a condom for their mutual protection. The relatively rare use of birth control, then, is a reflection of, among other things, these young girls' ambivalence about whether it is appropriate to have sex in the first place.

Their discomfiture is manifested in many other ways. Ask a teenager if she has ever taken a mirror to see what her own genitals look like, and she is appalled. Most girls are less comfortable touching themselves "down there" than they are allowing a boy the same favor. One nurse practitioner with whom I spoke has seen a parade of young women with downcast eyes who report all the classic symptoms of pregnancy — nausea, sore breasts, water retention — induced by nothing more than morning-after guilt. A loving, accepting mother says she is well aware that her daughter is having sexual relations with her boyfriend, but the girl is, nevertheless, too embarrassed to watch an R-rated movie with her, and is outraged when poor old Mom swims nude in the family pool.

Teenagers themselves often voice confusion and ambivalence about their sexuality. "I don't think I feel guilty about having sex," says an attractive blonde, fifteen, who has "slept with" two boys. "But then sometimes I start to wonder if the guy is taking advantage of me — or even if am taking advantage of him. That does bother me."

What else should we know about the sexually active teenage girl? She might be anyone's daughter, although when it comes to the statistics, she is more likely to belong to some of us than others. A rough sketch, admittedly drawn in broad strokes, from a number of studies on the subject tells us that besides the fact that the girl who has waved her virginity good-bye is not completely comfortable with her new "womanly" status, she tends to have lower self-esteem than either the sexually inexperienced girl or the sexually active boy.

She is not particularly religious, nor does she go to church unless her parents coax her. She is especially sensitive to group pressure, and her friends also tend to be sexually experienced. She is more likely than her less sexually experienced peers to experiment with drugs or alcohol. She may feel as if she can't talk easily to her parents, or she might come from a home where discipline is inconsistent, or from a one-parent family.

Her parents are somewhat less likely than the parents of more sexually reticent girls to have high educational aspirations for her. And, if we can take the source at face value, apparently, she is not likely to be class president; in a poll conducted by *Who's Who Among American High School Students,* 70 percent of the high achievers and student leaders claimed they had never had intercourse; more than half said they preferred to marry a virgin; and only about a third approved of premarital sex at all.

And in a seeming paradox, researchers have concluded that rather than being a standard-bearer for liberation of women, the sexually active girl is more likely to believe in traditional females' roles. How is that? Apparently girls who have sex early do so primarily to please a boy, while the girls who abstain until they are older are more intent on first attending to their own needs. According to one study, the high school girls who were still virgins, but who could foresee changing that status when the time was right for them — with or without benefit of the marriage vows — were judged to be more independent than the girls who lost their virginity early.

And just as in the good old, bad old days, our daughters are often continuing to play follow-the-leader when it comes to where and when they will have sex. "They pretty much still see boys as the impresarios who orchestrate it all," says Peggy Golden. "They suffer the illusion that they are safer, morally, if they are not the ones making the decisions. Like many of their mothers, girls are hiding behind their dependence on the opposite sex."

It is not my intention nor my wish even to begin to arbitrate the morality of teenage sex. I think it is more reasonable and, I hope, more helpful for us as parents and friends to consider whether becoming sexually active adds to or substracts from a particular young woman's self-esteem, sense of wholeness, and appreciation of aliveness. Because sex, before an individual is emotionally equipped to handle the consequences, or sex for the "wrong" reasons, can turn out calamitously.

As psychologist Vivian Kaplan says: "Teenage sex per se is not unhealthy. What it's used for can be — like trying to control other human beings, to put another individual or yourself down, to try to fit in to the group mold, or to convince yourself that 'I'm OK,' when you don't already know it."

Unfortunately, there are plenty of girls who have sex because they don't feel as if they have a place of their own in their own families. They are lonely, and they badly need to belong somewhere, even if in the arms of a boy, and if only for an hour or so. These girls are not hungry for sexual stimulation but for cuddling and stroking and a very basic kind of acceptance which they somehow missed out on along the way to adolescence. And if they can't get acceptance, many will settle for attention.

"Some girls think there is nothing they can do to win their parents' acceptance, so it doesn't make much difference if they do something as unacceptable as having sex.

At least they might be noticed," says Bob Iles, with sadness. "And if they haven't found real meaning in the relationship with their parents, maybe — just maybe — they can find it in this new one."

Marcy Graham is a teacher and a mother of a seventeen-year-old. "I recently walked around Katy's high school campus, and felt this tremendous wave of aloneness and falseness from girls and boys who seemed to be trying to be something they didn't truly feel. It appears to me that they use sex to fill in the blanks."

Another "bad" reason to become sexually active? That old devil, peer pressure. Most teenagers have not been liberated from the intense peer pressure to drink, to smoke pot, to have sex. The same sort of pressure that used to drive girls not to have sex is now driving them to it. Peer pressure used to dictate "Good girls don't"; now girls feel there is something physically or emotionally wrong with them if they graduate from high school without also graduating from the state of virginity. Sex has become the new initiation rite. The tragedy is — liberation be damned — that so many girls don't think they have the right to answer in the negative when a boy proposes "going all the way."

If they say "no" now, some are even afraid they may be frigid or neurotic or will look like inexperienced fools when the "right" men come along. (Boys worry that they may not be "real men.") Because the very young are so vulnerable and inexperienced, outside influences can be very effective in making them doubt their own best instincts.

"I haven't had sex yet," defensively says sixteen-year-old Jenny. "I hate to reject a boy I really like, but sometimes I want to scream, 'This is my body — get your hands off it.' And though I guess it's silly, sometimes I wonder if something is wrong with me. Maybe I should be more turned on.

"I sure like to cuddle and kiss, but spending hours making out with a guy just doesn't hold a lot of interest for me yet. Still, sometimes I think it would be easier to just give in. So many other girls do."

Girls need a lot of encouragement if they are to resist having sex before they are ready. "No" can be a difficult word when "yes" appears to be so much more popular and, on the surface, so much more rewarding. (In the next chapter, I'll look at how you can help them see the value of and feel more comfortable with saying that difficult two-letter word.)

What is the price these teenagers could pay for becoming sexually experienced before they are really ready? Some experts say that too-early sexual involvement, which is often egocentric and immature, can impede the growth of later partnerships of greater depth and maturity. And for girls, who still tend to become much more dependent on their sexual partners, sex before attaining some measure of selfhood may actually delay independence (and real liberation). And experts are also fearful that sexually precocious young people may suffer sexual dysfunction, including impotence and frigity, somewhere down the road. (Which is funny — painfully so, since young people think they will become those things if they don't test out their equipment early on.)

There may also be short-term psychic penalties.

"I worry about some of these kids who become sexual so young," says Shari Glucoft-Wong. "They say to me, 'I thought I was okay but I don't know if I can handle this anymore. I sleep with this guy, and I don't know why, but afterward it hurts a lot more if he lets me down, or isn't there for me when I think I need him.'

"Like it or not, sexuality does lead to increased vulnerability, and many of these girls don't have the resources to handle that."

When teenagers — or any of us, for that matter — don't understand their own feelings or values, they tend to "act out," perhaps hoping that having sex will provide that understanding. But often that only creates new complications.

"When a young girl has sex without knowing what it means to her, she is essentially cutting her feelings off from her body, so that she doesn't have to face the fact that she is putting herself through something she is not at all sure she believes in," says Fern Rubin. "But because being a virgin is not generally a popular position to maintain, she may relinquish that undesirable status without thinking about it. Then she has to hide the guilt and anxiety, the headaches and the hives she gets from not being who she truly is."

And if we are to help our daughters perceive themselves as whole, loving, and sexual persons — who are not compelled to act out that sexuality to meet needs that would best be met in other ways — we need to be aware, once again, that they are growing up in a time and place that send them continually conflicting messages about what is right and wrong.

For instance, there is the pretense that when it comes to sexuality, boys and girls are equals. But, as was already made clear by the horrendous inequality of our juvenile justice system in its punishment of youthful female sexuality, we still cling tenaciously to a double standard. We still still find it much easier to accept our sons as sexual beings.

And as therapist and researcher Peggy Golden points out, we still teach our daughters to value being the object of love and our sons to value action and conquests. We still set up different standards for their behavior. If it appears that a young girl is behaving like a male — in this case, sexual — we simply say she is bad, though we may not say it as loudly as we would have a few years ago.

A number of studies show that many parents are more tolerant of any kind of sexual behavior — from masturbation, to light petting, to intercourse — when their sons, rather than daughters, are the perpetrators. A Gallup Youth Survey of teenagers reveals that girls are more likely to be handed a curfew on dates, to be limited in the number of times a week they can go out, and to hear parental objections about whom they are going out with. A Los Angeles *Times* poll found that while parents were not crazy about the idea of any child of theirs having sex under their roofs, they were more likely to refuse a daughter the license.

Bob Iles calls it the King of Siam syndrome: "The bee shall go from flower to flower, but the flower shall not go from bee to bee."

Our double standard seems to indicate that we still cling to outmoded ideas that sexual experience makes our daughters used goods, and even subtracts from their "value" in the marital marketplace. And biology does make it easier to ignore the evidence of our sons' sexual activity, for if a daughter gets pregnant, the whole world knows you have been harboring a sexually active child.

We may also be fearful for our girls, because we continue to think that women, in both tangible and intangible ways, are hurt through sex. "If you pin down the most intelligent, sophisticated woman, you'll still find she is afraid of her daughter's being manipulated, exploited, and injured through her sexuality," points out Peggy Golden.

And though our daughters are hearing that, as women,

they now have much greater control over their destinies than did their foremothers, how many of us are still more accepting of our daughter's sexual escapade if she has been overwhelmed with passion or swept off her feet than if there was foresight and planning involved. "She couldn't help herself," or "He made her do it," we can console ourselves — thus reinforcing the old stereotype of the helpless female who was overpowered by the male animal. (An attitude that, as we shall see later, does much to encourage intercourse without consciousness or protection.)

On the other hand, the double standard dictates that a "good girl" must be the strong one who puts the brakes on when passion begins to get the upper hand. And in the enlightened eighties, the age-old dichotomy of the "good girl" and the "bad girl" is still alive and doing nicely.

In many instances, teenagers themselves have bought heavily into the double standard. In a 1980 study, jointly sponsored by UCLA and the Rand Corporation, 54 percent of boys and 42 percent of girls, ranging in age from fourteen to eighteen, agreed that if a girl "leads a boy on" or "gets him sexually excited," but then changes her mind about having sex, the boy has the right to use force on her. And the female, say these teenagers, is the responsible party.

Many of these young people also thought that it "might" be okay for a boy to force himself on a girl if they have had sex before, if they dated regularly, if she has had sex with other boys, or if she accepts an invitation to a party where she knows there will be liquor or drugs. The boys who were surveyed agreed that any girl who wears tight jeans or goes bra-less was definitely advertising her sexual availability. But on the other side of the double standard, no one took it a sexual cue when a boy wore tight pants or had a proclivity toward leaving several buttons on his shirt undone.

And, even though such social arbiters as Ann Landers and Emily Post say it's now acceptable for a girl to call a boy, most males in the UCLA-Rand study say they interpret a telephone call from a girl as a sign that she is "willing" to have sex. (The girls, fortunately, said "no" to this one.)

Many teenage girls, like Elizabeth, protest the inequity, but don't feel they have the power to change it. Elizabeth is a bright sixteen-year-old with Alice-in-Wonderland hair and, according to today's skewered standards, a slightly tarnished reputation. "In my crowd, a 'good' girl manages to keep what she does quiet. "A 'bad' girl," she says, with more than a trace of bitterness, "is one who sleeps around just enough so that the word gets out. I get mad whenever I realize there's no such thing as 'good' boys and 'bad' boys — just those who are experienced and inexperienced.

"Boys pressure you to have sex, and then a lot of them turn around and brand you with a bad rep after you have given in to them. You can't win."

Boys and girls apparently still have different expectations of sex, love, and romance. In most surveys, girls rank romance higher than sex, while the opposite is true for boys. "Girls want to fall in love. Boys want to fall into sex," giggles a fifteen-year-old philosopher after recounting a backseat battle with an eighteen-year-old "man." "For girls, sex is sort of sacred. For guys, it's fun and it's also something they've got to do."

When questioned by Gallup pollsters, more girls than boys said they were "in love" and "going steady." (Does this mean that some girls are going out with faithless fellows?) On the other hand, more boys claimed they kiss on first dates. Other studies show that, for boys, first intercourse is more likely to occur with a casual partner, which leads researchers to conclude that young males plan for short-run sexual success, while young females are more interested in long-term relationships. Sixty percent of the 1,000 boys in a New York study said it was kosher to tell a girl they loved her if the object was to encourage her to have sex with them.

None of the above signifies, of course, that the adolescent females of the species are finer human beings than are members of the other sex. As we've already said, the sexes have always been conditioned differently: men to make their mark and score points, women to base their self-worth on the quality of their intimate relationships.

Things are only beginning to change, including this bulletin to be heard from the teenage male consciousness-raising front: "Many boys today are becoming extremely sensitive and caring," says Maurie Cullen. "They talk about their dissatisfaction with the stereotypical male as a sexual, social, and work performer. They are saying they can't become sexually involved with a girl they don't care about. Of course, they might not admit that to their peers because they feel like they're in a minority."

But that is a start.

Our daughters are not the only ones going through a time of sexual upheaval. So are their mothers. I hope that this chapter has helped to open up some understanding of what younger women are going through on the sexual front. The next chapter also addresses *you* as a sexual person, and examines the promise of both mothers' and daughters' becoming more comfortable and lovingly expressive around their sexuality.

# 6

## A Few Words on Getting Both of You through the Sexual Wars

WALKING THE FLOOR WITH HER all night when she was cutting teeth was easy compared to waiting out her puberty. The endless procession of skinned knees, even broken bones, occasional bad report cards, the terrible twos, the lonely sevens, the belligerent nines, or whatever developmental problems our singularly gifted daughters had — all pieces of cake, when compared to being asked to acknowledge and accept her as a sexual person.

Especially in times that challenge her to express her sexuality before she may be ready, when the general tendancy is to cleave unto short-run solutions like the Pill, rather than putting any thought into what is most intelligent and loving, not just now, but over the long haul. Especially when the word is that "Everybody is doing it, so what's wrong with you, anyway?"

And it is also difficult to go through this transition with her because her flowering tells us so much about ourselves, things we may not always be comfortable knowing or remembering. At times, we may see her growth as a consummation of our own, a natural and joyful part of life's cycle. We may be proud of her bloom, yet anxious about what she chooses to do with it; regretful at the passing of our own youth, jealous she has all of the good times ahead of her. Suddenly, we must confront all of our own beliefs and values and still-unanswered questions about sex, and about other of life's stubborn mysteries.

Sex may be the issue that forces us to see that our child is no longer a child. We may come up against the reality that, barring locking her in her room until she reaches eighteen, there is little we can do to control her sexuality. And we may not like that fact of life one bit.

As she becomes preoccupied with the changes in her body, our own middle-aged metamorphoses are upon us. An unfair double-decker rite of passage, a sort of handing down the flame of fertility, symbolized by menarche and menopause, inconsiderately scheduled by Ma Nature to coincide.

While the commercial may say it's better you're getting, not older, the thought is small consolation when we live in a culture that puts such a high premium on youth.

"If your self-image is not the greatest, if you have seen your body get a bit flabby, and suddenly this firm, voluptuous young thing is living amongst the family," asks Maurie Cullen, "who can blame you for being threatened and depressed?

"And if you believe you are losing your physical attractiveness, it's common for you to feel less valuable in other ways. I know a number of women who also have begun to feel stupid and helpless right about this time."

Jealousy, envy, and the urge to compete with our daughters are par for the course now, and there are plenty of "normal" women who at one time or another, when contemplating their daughters, have found themselves wishing very fervently that Ponce de Leon had been more persistent in his fountainless search.

• "The way she's blooming makes me take a harder look at my image. I'm getting . . . well, older. We certainly aren't one of those cute mother-daughter pairs you see on TV whom everyone says look more like sisters. I definitely look like Mary's mother. In fact, sometimes when I look at her tan, firm body — a body that can eat anything and do without sleep and still have endless energy — I feel more like her grandmother. At those moments I hate her."

• "I ask myself: how did she suddenly take the spotlight? I'm not ready to be relegated to the backseat. But then I feel like the wicked stepmother in those fairy tales, the ones who were always trying to feed the innocent, beautiful young girl the poison apple."

• "I'm embarrassed. The last few times she got all dressed up to go out, I wasn't sharing in her excitement. I was jealous. She has so much ahead of her, and my time feels like it's running out."

Please know that the feelings of jealousy and competition are absolutely normal, though most of us are too embarrassed to admit those green-eyed gremlins could be there. In the first place, haven't we learned somewhere that competition itself is unfeminine? And in the second place — and more to the point — it seems unnatural and unloving to have such unattractive emotions around the little person we have borne and raised.

Nevertheless, on some level, we frequently find ourselves competing with those not-so-little women who are our daughters. A rivalry between mother and daughter for the attention of the man of the house is one of the most common manifestations of this competition. And how much more difficult it makes it for us that this is often the time when a father becomes more interested in his daughter as a companion, and even becomes threatened by the boys her own age who show an interest in her.

"When I see Katy and Sam go off together I start getting these really possessive thoughts, thoughts that freak me out," says Marcy Graham. "I recognize that it's irrational, but I get a feeling I'm being replaced, that neither of them needs me.

"I know that Sam sees Katy's body as exciting and new and young, and I know that he used to see my body the same way. But after eighteen years of marriage, that has worn off.

"I can understand how people have affairs during these years. You pick up on the sexuality of the young, and you want to fall in love and be swept off your feet again."

What's a mother to do about her jealousy? First, accept it as normal. And then, as clinical psychologist Marilyn Mehr advises, you can let your daughter know — gently — that Mom and Dad are from one generation and she is from another, and she needn't feel she must compete for his attention. Because the father-husband, if he is a loving individual, has plenty of love to give to both of them. Of course, if the daughter is to understand that, her mother must also believe that that is, indeed, the truth.

And while it is normal to envy your daughter her youth and blooming sexuality, it is possible to move past that. "I used to be frightfully jealous of Jordon," says one mother. "But then, I began to realize — with the support of some loving women friends, that there is more to life than being fifteen. In my own way, I am blooming, too. I think I am more attractive and vital at forty-two than I was at twenty-two. The aging process no longer means gray hair, lines, and flab. For me, it signals maturity, exposure to life, experience. I haven't really missed out on anything, it's just that liberation is a change-of-life phenomenon for me."

It is easy to see how problems in marriages can come to the surface for the first time during a child's adolescence. (Even affairs, where before fidelity had been complete, are not uncommon during this time.) Her emerging sexuality makes it more difficult to look away from issues that may have long been pushed into a corner. You may, apparently all of a sudden, be dissatisfied that you have settled for less than satisfaction.

Marriages may need extra nurturing now. As Maurie Cullen pointed out to me, over the years, couples often become so busy making money and raising a family, they forget how to have fun, and even forget that they originally got together because they were interested in, and in love with, each other. She counsels parents of teenagers to find time to be together, away from their children, learn to share a hobby or go off on a weekend.

Also, teenagers are not the only ones who need peer group support. Parents, caught up in the drama of raising an adolescent, might find it really helpful to become involved with people their own age.

Your daughter's transition into womanhood might even be a positive stimulus for your relationship with your husband, as one mother describes. "When Mindy began to be aware of boys and to date, Dave and I found we had more time alone together," recounts Deborah, a trim woman with frosted hair and twinkling eyes. "At first, we didn't know what to talk about or what to do. For the first time in a lot of years we felt we didn't have to worry about Mindy or her two older brothers. We had confidence that they would be all right without us hovering over them.

"Dave and I started to notice each other again, like it was the first time. We've been going out on 'dates' like we used to. We have more time alone in the house since before we had the three kids. I am really enjoying this time."

It is not uncommon, nor is it unnatural, for parents to experience sexual feelings that *seem* aimed toward their adolescent children or their children's friends.

"Sometimes I notice I'm flirting with Sandy's boyfriends," said one mother. "They're really cute. Am I a silly old woman?"

And another mother: "Once in a while, I feel a turn-on when I am around my own teenage daughters. I finally realized that those feelings are a waking-up of my own sexuality, rekindled, I suppose, by the emergence of my daughters' sexuality."

Fathers have similar feelings, and are, says Bob Iles, "enormously relieved" when he assures them such feelings are common and natural.

"All sexual feelings are pleasurable and they are all valid, but we don't act on all of them. If we ask ourselves if it is appropriate to be sexually intimate with a child or with a parent, the answer will be 'no.' "

But the young woman who knows that her father accepts her as an attractive, sexual being will be less likely to need to prove it elsewhere before she is ready. "When I was an adolescent, and I wanted an easy makeout, I'd deliberately choose girls who didn't have fathers, or who were alienated from their fathers," says Iles. "They needed to know they were attractive and lovable, so I found they were always available."

With all of this confronting us, is it any wonder then that we will often avoid, until we can avoid no longer, recognizing this new sexual being in our midst? And there are endless ways we can pull the wool over our eyes. Consider Emmy Anders, a *not* unliberated lady when it comes to having a job she loves or making sure that household chores are distributed fairly among all family members. Emmy even made sure she told her daughter about the "birds and the bees" when Toni was eight, but she never quite got around to telling Toni about the men and the women and the boys and the girls. The Anders family lives in what they like to think of as a "liberal" community, and Emmy told herself that her cute, popular fifteen-year-old daughter learned in school everything she needed to know about sex.

When it occurred to Emmy at all to bring up the subject of sex to a daughter whose bra was a cup size larger than her own, she shrugged off the idea. "I figured that, with the way kids grow up so fast nowadays, Toni would just laugh at me. I was sure she could teach me a thing or two.

"And besides," she added with a very small smile, "I was too embarrassed."

Another mother tells me — also as if she needs to defend herself: "We don't really come out and discuss sex per se, but everybody in our house feels free to kid around about it. Wouldn't you call that 'openness'?"

Unfortunately, sex is one of those subjects about which everyone does a lot of assuming (and acting upon and "kidding around about") but little real communicating. Not only is there a great deal of embarrassment, but mothers and daughters often think they need to protect each other from the truth.

In separate interviews, Trudy and Shirley Goldberg initially agreed that sex is a wide-open topic in their household. "I'm totally honest with her — except for the few things I don't think she could handle," explains daughter Trudy. "I would like her to know I am not a virgin, but I don't want to hit her with it until she's ready. Sometimes she needs protection."

Mother Shirley, for her part, thinks Trudy *is* telling her

everything. "Sex is considered healthy in my house, and it's a no-holds-barred topic. I have a Picasso nude in the bedroom, and together Trudy and I have looked at a *Hustler* magazine in the grocery store."

Shirley thinks any embarrassment in their relationship belongs to her daughter. "I don't ask her whether she and Jon are having a sexual side to their relationship. She would be too uncomfortable to tell me."

But when pressed further, Shirley Goldberg, like Emmy Anders, like so many mothers, admits that there is not a lot of open, give-and-take discussion with her daughter about the issues and the information around sexuality. Who is protecting whom, from what?

Some parents excuse the lack of in-home openness by assuming that their kids learn in school all they need to be sexually informed. That is a faulty, even a dangerous, assumption because only a handful of states even require sex education or family-life classes as part of the classroom curriculum. Those classes that are offered usually concentrate on social diseases and basic biology. Comparatively few look at issues like birth control or the risks to young girls who become pregnant and have babies. Fewer still discuss relationships between people, the psychological and social consequences of early sexuality, or offer genuine dialogue between teachers and students.

"Sex education in most schools is as close to irrelevant as it can be," says Bob Iles.

But no matter how good, the school and its sex education program should never be the first or the last word on the subject. A young girl needs to be able to talk to her parents about her feelings and concerns. According to a study from the Merrill-Palmer Institute of Detroit, the relationship between mother and daughter is more significant than any other factor — including race, religion, socioeconomic class, and even her parents' marital status — when predicting a girl's sexual attitudes and behavior.

In fact, girls who are close to their mothers, says the study, are more likely to be virgins or at least to be more sexually "responsible" than the girls who are on distant terms with their mothers.

Some parents hold back from openly discussing sexuality with their teenagers because they are afraid that talking would be tantamount to making an all-out endorsement of the act itself. And often that fear is based on the belief that once our daughters have sex, they are somehow lost to us, almost as if their molecules will rearrange themselves in a completely unfamiliar — and unreachable — configuration. That is not true, and yet our attitudes often change markedly toward those we know to be sexually active, and that goes double when our own daughters are involved.

"The day before a girl has her first sexual experience and the day after, she isn't two different people," says Fern Rubin. "Sex doesn't transform us. But we pass that idea on to our children. Most girls will tell you — if they're honest — they were disappointed with their first time, disappointed because they thought the world would suddenly be different. My daughter said to me, 'Maybe I should have sex now and settle the whole issue.' And I answered, 'Sure, and you'll have four other — probably hairier — issues to settle right after that.'"

Because of their own discomfort with matters sexual, some mothers try to pretend their daughters' sexuality doesn't exist at all. While they may not be aware they are doing it, they closely guard information about sex and birth control, ignore clues that their daughters need guidance, and conceal evidence of their own sexuality by never talking about it or not expressing affection with their mates.

A few mothers, again because they have never found it easy to accept themselves as sexual persons, may punish their daughters for reminding them. One young girl told me that, after she got pregnant and told her mother she wanted to keep her baby, her mother not only "forced" her to have an abortion, but then made her do the family grocery shopping two hours after the procedure was performed.

But most of the mothers with whom I talked are concerned whether or not they are setting an example that will contribute to a healthy and whole expression of sexuality in their daughters.

• "I've wanted to be a good sexual role model for Karen. I want her to know that sex has been a very positive experience for me and that I'm comfortable with my sexuality, but that sometimes I, too, get involved in sex for invalid reasons. Like the times I'd like affection and intimacy but not necessarily sex, but I end up going through the 'act' to get to the other things. At those times, sex is not that fulfilling."

• "My mother gave me the message that she didn't enjoy sex. My father believed sex was a wonderful thing. Since my father was a more alive, turned-on person, I chose to believe him.

"I'd like Kendra to know what I learned from my father."

• "I was scared the first time I had sex. I wasn't ready. It was too fast and not loving enough. I didn't even know what orgasms were, but I remembered thinking, 'Can *this* be it?' I want Linda to understand that sex gets better with time and patience."

Single mothers have special concerns about whether they are good sexual models for their daughters. Some believe it is better if they keep their relationships with men completely separate from their home lives. Others think it helps their daughters to let them know their mothers have loving, sexual relationships with men.

• "Since the divorce, I haven't brought a lover to the house. Even though their father left me, my girls resent other men in my life, so I keep those two parts of my life completely separate.

"As a consequence, I haven't had many lovers. Friends are wonderful, but they can't reach out and hold you in the middle of the night. I'd like a man I can sleep with, a man with integrity and intelligence, who can make me laugh.

"But I'll wait until my kids are grown and out of the house before I really resume that part of my life."

• "In my day, and especially in my Catholic family, sex before marriage was an unpardonable sin. I got married at seventeen to get away. My relationship with Lisa's father was not particularly loving, and I wasn't a good model for her when I was married.

"Since my divorce, Lisa has found out that it's possible to have loving relationships with men — relationships that may include sexuality. Lisa and I are growing up together."

Some mothers hold back because they are afraid to discover just how different their attitudes about sex may be from their daughters'. But who has ever said that mothers and daughters have to agree?

If you have never really talked to your daughter about sex, it won't be easy to start now. But, despite a recent Harvard study that intimates that parents who haven't talked to their kids about sex by the age of eleven might as well not bother, now is still better than not at all. And be assured that just as asking a depressed teenager if she is thinking about harming herself will not lead her to suicide, telling your daughter you are open to discussing sexual issues will not lead to rampant promiscuity. On the contrary, she must first have information and an opportunity for dialogue even to begin to behave ethically. How can she decide what to do if she doesn't know what the options are?

If you ask almost any teenager what sort of information she wants from her mother, very likely it won't be about birth control or anything to do with the technical side of sex, but about the link between physical intimacy and love, the meaning of responsibility to another person or to a new life, whether her erotic fantasies are normal, and advice on refusing a too-eager suitor.

Following are some ideas on beginning a dialogue on sexuality, gathered from experts and from mothers and daughters.

• If your daughter asks you a sex-related question, answer *that* question, and don't immediately conclude that she *really* means something else. For instance, if she asks you if birth control pills are safe, try to help her find the answer to that question before jumping to the angry conclusion that she is already taking them. Once you've answered her initial question, you might — if she is receptive — ask if she is aware of the meaning of asking the question. But try not to accuse her or badger her.

She needs you to trust her, and to remind her that you are always there for the asking — even though the answers might not always be easy or even possible.

• If you sense that she does have other questions behind her questions, but that she isn't comfortable broaching them now, tell her that you will be receptive when she is ready.

• Let her know you believe in her — if that is, indeed, so — and are more concerned with the quality of her life and her relationships than with what she did on her date last night. As one mother told her daughter: "You may stick up a bank or get pregnant, but I want you to remember you will always be my kid."

• If you are embarrassed, or unclear yourself, tell her. No one expects mothers to be without doubt or ambivalence about such a charged topic, or to be the final authority. It's OK to tell a young person, "I am not sure about this," or "I don't know what that means." The problems arise when you pretend you are sure or you do know, when you aren't and you don't, because if you are dishonest, with yourself or with your daughter about your discomfort with sexuality, *that* is when you will transmit mixed or unclear messages. Messages like "Sex is beautiful after you're twenty-one and married, but dirty until then," or "I want you to be free to enjoy your sexuality," while it's obvious that yours is in chains, can be confusing and even "crazymaking" for her.

"With such conflicting messages, the young woman will have a difficult time trusting her own impulses, or developing a sense of what is right or wrong for her," says psychologist Barbara Hayes.

She may also have trouble responding joyfully and openly to her own sexuality, or she may set herself up to be hurt through it. That way she can reassure herself that Mother did indeed know best, and she does not then risk losing your love. If she has sex despite your forebodings, now or even in a few years, she may keep the betrayal at least emotionally unconsummated by not enjoying it.

In short, it simply doesn't work to try to be someone you

aren't or to endorse a philosophy you honestly don't feel is a good one. *Tell her* if sex is an uncomfortable topic for you. It will be a tremendous relief for her to know that people — especially her mother — don't know it all and don't need to know it all to be happy and healthy. You might even be able to find someone else — a friend, a minister, even a trained counselor — to help you bridge the subject with your daughter.

And yet while it is important to be able to admit your uncertainty to yourself, and then to be able to acknowledge it to her, it is also necessary to continue to examine and try to understand your values. Be honest with yourself so you can be honest with her.

She needs to know what you believe in and she needs guidelines, even if you must risk seeming old-fashioned or heavy-handed. If you hold back, you are telling her, by omission, that sex is not a matter for thoughtful reflection.

"When Kathryn first began bringing her boyfriend over to study and they were spending a lot of time in her bedroom with the door closed, I wasn't comfortable telling her I was uncomfortable," explained Suzanne Gunderson. "It seemed pretty unenlightened of me. But finally I knew it was wrong to let her think I believed in something I didn't. I told her how I felt, and that while I realized it was not up to me when she would experience sex, I felt she wasn't ready at this time. Given that feeling, it didn't seem right to set it up for her, providing her with a bedroom with a locked door."

Many researchers would agree that Suzanne Gunderson probably contributed to Kathy's growth. For instance, while the previously mentioned Merrill-Palmer study also revealed that a girl's virginity had nothing to do with a mother's constant proctoring — waiting up for her, questioning her about where she was going and with whom — neither did a dearth of rules exercise the reverse psychology, necessarily encouraging her to hang on to her virginity. "A lot of today's adults feel that, as youngsters, they were damaged by antisexual religious and social dogma, and now they are leaning backward to be supportive of their own kids," says Peggy Golden.

"They think that means having no rules. But kids need strong guidelines — even if they are ultimately guidelines to react against and reject. They need that starting place."

On the other hand, it helps to know that neither does the measure of a good parent have a direct correlation with the amount of control she can exert over her child.

"If you have tight reins over your fifteen-year-old," says Bob Iles, "you've actually failed as a parent, because the goal of parenting is to help create a mature person with a sound system of values who can make healthy choices and who will be a contribution to the lives of everyone around her."

Marcy Graham has found that life does seem to work more harmoniously when she doesn't keep arbitrary "tight reins" on her daughter, but instead allows her to see more clearly the consequences of her actions.

"I have learned that if I am bothered by a tight sweater or pair of shorts Katy is wearing, I don't tell her not to wear it. Instead, I might say, 'If you want to be seen as sexy and are willing to take responsibility for that, then go ahead and wear what you've got on.'

"That way, we are both clear on what's going on. And oftentimes she won't say anything, but she changes into something more appropriate."

• Sharing your own experience can also be a helpful — and loving — thing to do. "This happened to me. . . ."

"How confused I was when . . ." As one mother says, openness must be a two-way street. "I can't expect her to tell me about her sexuality and then presume to totally hide my own. I want her to feel free to ask about my first sexual experience or whether or not I have had an affair — which does not mean I'd always feel comfortable answering her questions."

Real openness — not the sort of brutal honesty that can be a verbal sledgehammer — is important to both mother and daughter.

"The more my daughter opens up and talks to me about what she is feeling and experiencing, the more comfortable I am, because those experiences and feelings are comfortable to me; they are known to me," says Fern Rubin. "It's OK with me if she has secrets. I only get uptight when I sense she feels guilty or uncomfortable about what she isn't saying. If she is open, at least open enough to let me know that she feels comfortable in keeping a part of her life private, then I'm OK, and I don't have to impose my own meanings on what I imagine is going on with her."

Many a young woman today is, on the one hand, torn between her society's rather obvious insinuation that if she doesn't become sexually active now, there's something wrong with her, and on the other, by her own instinct, which may tell her she isn't ready yet to take on the responsibility that goes with the act.

If a young girl does not have a clear understanding that she is ready to have sex, she probably isn't, and you can help her to see that there is absolutely nothing wrong with her on that count. Share with her what you have learned about how hurtful sex can be when the time and the person are inappropriate.

And it would definitely benefit all concerned if we, as mothers and wives and persons, could look at our own ideas about that tiny little word — "no." So many of us have a tough time saying it — especially to a member of the other sex — that it shouldn't be surprising when our daughters inherit that particular difficulty from us.

As Fern Rubin says, "If my daughter has grown up watching me trying to have an effect on the man in my life by constantly doing or saying what I think will please him, that is what she will do."

For, women's liberation notwithstanding, girls are still having sex to please their boyfriends. They are afraid that, as one girl put it, "He won't be around much longer if I don't have sex with him. I don't want to be left out in the cold, so I am going to do it."

We have always believed that, as females, when we are good — that is, when we refrain from saying "no" — we can keep the people we care about or depend on from leaving us. That is the stance of a victim, someone who sees the world as a basically unstable, hostile place, someone who needs to hold on tightly to others in order to stay afloat.

Which girls have an advantage when it comes to being able to give "no" for an answer? The girl who is growing up in a home where her parents see the world as a good, safe place; where she is told that the choices she is free to make can make it an even better place; where she is allowed to express a variety of emotions, and where anger and depression are not seen as crazy aunts that need to be kept hidden away in the attic.

"I don't worry about Lisa buckling under to pressure," says Lisa's mother. "The first word she ever learned was 'no.' She has always had permission to voice her opinions and feelings. We don't always agree, and there are certainly times I exercise my judgment as her mother and overrule her. But I never pretend that I have the corner on the market for knowing better than she does what is best for her.''

When *is* a very young woman emotionally ready to be actively sexual? First and foremost, she should like herself and know that she deserves good things and that she has something to offer the world. Then it's important for her to have a relationship with a boy who she knows is not interested in compromising or degrading her, who knows who she is and appreciates her gifts.

It might be helpful for anyone considering a sexual relationship to ask themselves some thoughtful questions, questions like: Who *is* this person I am considering sharing something very precious with? Is his way of looking at the world compatible with mine? What sorts of expectations are we bringing to this experience, and are they based in reality? Does being physically intimate mean the same thing to both of us? Am I contemplating adding a new dimension to this relationship because he is a special human being, or because the way he looks and acts impresses people and makes *me* look important?

How will sex change the nature of our relationship? Will we still feel as comfortable with each other? How will he feel if we have sex, and then break up? How will I feel?

We also need to question whether we can handle the social consequences of our sexuality: How will others — parents, girl friends, other boys — regard us if they know we are having sex? Will we be accepted? Will we jeopardize other relationships?

Another essential question is: What kind of birth control should I obtain? And where will I get it? (See chapter 8 on contraception.)

There are other questions to be asked, which may seem far afield from the sexual issue at hand, but are very much to the point: What does it mean to love and care for another? What is trust? Loyalty? Selfishness? What is the difference between loving and being loved, and using and being used?

After carefully considering questions like these, some girls may decide — responsibly — to become sexually active.

• "I will know I'm ready to have sex when I can talk fairly easily about my feelings and experiences with my mother, and ask her to help me get birth control. I guess, in a way, that's asking for her acceptance, but that's still important to me."

• "I think I'm becoming ready for sex. I used to feel afraid of becoming involved, or uncomfortable with the thought of being undressed in front of someone. I guess I'm not afraid of those things anymore, and I've accepted that my body isn't perfect, but that doesn't matter so much to me. And it won't matter to someone who really cares about me."

• "I'd really like to experience something special with someone I care about. For me, it isn't that I want to have my first experience to get it out of the way. I used to think that after the first time, I would be past some big hurdle and it would be no big deal when I came to the next person. But I realize I'll be confronting the same issues each time. If it is right with one boy, it doesn't mean it will be right with the next one."

There comes a point at which you can no longer protect your daughter. And when a "child" becomes an adolescent, a good deal of what you believe is already instilled in her. You can't ride in the backseat when she goes out on dates, but you can know that she is going to take a part of you with her.

When she chooses to get sexually involved with another

human being, she may make mistakes. And she may get hurt. All of us do. But you can't hold her back from experiencing life. And you shouldn't want to. That's not your job.

# 7

## *Birth Control: Is Anyone Responsible?*

"I THINK IN MOST WAYS we understand each other. We've had our little talks about sex. I know we don't always agree on certain areas, but I can handle that, I think. However, I don't know what to do — if anything — about birth control."

That is a not-at-all-uncommon motherly reaction to the subject of contraception. Even if you are the kind of mother she can come to when she isn't sure whether "no" is good enough, or "yes" is better still. Even if you no longer impose your values on her. Even if you have smiled bravely when a date picks her up in a Winnebago with the bumper sticker that proclaims, "Don't come a-knockin' when this van's a-rockin'."

Your liberation mask still slips a little when it comes to birth control. What *do* you do when it comes to making sure she is protecting herself (and *you* from premature grandmotherhood)? Does helping her get birth control start her on the road to sexual junkiedom? Does she need your unsolicited advice, or should you stay mum on the whole subject and assume that, when she's ready, she will be mature enough to pick her own pill or diaphragm or whatever?

Before looking at those questions, let's step back and consider some other issues around birth control, like how the numbers of girls having sex and the numbers who are protecting themselves against pregnancy don't match up. Not at all.

A 1975 survey from the Alan Guttmacher Institute (AGI), a research organization that concentrates on social and political trends, revealed that, of over 4,000,000 sexually active girls between fifteen and nineteen in this country, fewer than 2,500,000 received contraceptive services from family-planning clinics and from private doctors.

That leaves at least a million and a half girls who are having unprotected intercourse or are using "drugstore" methods — which many teenagers have a record of using haphazardly. The result? According to various studies, around 60 percent of the girls who ignore birth control will get pregnant.

Many of the young women who do use birth control don't use it consistently: the Population Institute reports that only 30 percent of unmarried sexually active teenage women use contraception with any regularity.

So, once again, it's apparent that teens are not as liberated as rumor has had it, because while contraception *is* there, many seem to be harboring some big hang-ups about using it. It appears that the popular notion that "the Pill" has been one of the prime forces in the liberation of women over the last generation applies only when sexuality is viewed as a genuine mode of self-expression and personhood. For many teenagers, as we have already seen, the expression of sexuality has not yet reached that plane.

Therefore, for them, the responsible use of birth control has very little to do with freedom or liberation because those are not yet valid issues for them.

Specifically, I have found that young women have four areas of reluctance when it comes to using contraception.

First of all, many are not sufficiently adult (granted, a lot of adults are not that adult, either) to know enough about how their bodies work to put the brakes on procreation. Second, some really believe that they are immune to ending up as a statistic in the pregnancy, abortion, or teenage motherhood columns. Third, some are so uncomfortable with having sex they must have it unthinkingly (which lets out planning for protection). And, fourth, there are those, as we shall see, who *want* to have children.

There are many ways to be ignorant about contraception. Talking to pregnant teenagers — and teenagers who had terminated their pregnancies — I heard remarks like: "Everybody told me it couldn't happen your first time, because the first time is about losing your virginity and the next time you're clear for getting pregnant." (Actually, doesn't there seem to be something almost logical, albeit perversely so, about that one?) Or, "I didn't think I had had sex enough times to get pregnant." Along the same lines: "I have a diaphragm, but I don't always use it. I figured I used it often enough."

Then there are the girls who think protection is unnecessary because they confine their sexual activity to the "safe" times of the month. But a 1978 study conducted by sociologists Melvin Zelnik and John Kantner, of Johns Hopkins University, found that only two in five teenage girls had even the slightest idea when the risk of pregnancy was greatest.

Girls have also bought the horror stories — some with a

basis in fact — about the dangers of some forms of contraception. The Pill gives you cancer or, worse, makes you fat. The IUD makes you sterile. Apparently no one ever told them that when you are very young, carrying and delivering a baby is a much riskier proposition. (More about that later.)

"I was scared of birth control," said a seventeen-year-old with two abortions behind her. "I knew a girl whose face broke out when when she took the Pill. The IUD sounded just too weird — I mean putting a piece of wire in your stomach — yuk. No way would I walk into a drugstore and ask the guy there for something. And I just couldn't ask my boyfriend. He might not respect me if I couldn't take care of myself."

Some girls, despite our communications satellites and networks of computers, simply are ignorant of where to get birth control. "I wouldn't know where to go, and neither would my friends," said an obviously bright young woman with an academic average of B and a debatable D-minus in worldliness. And still others may know *where* to get contraception, but they would rather chance pregnancy than risk their parents' finding the evidence of their sexuality. So they get nothing.

In the it-can't-happen-to-me school, there is the line of thinking that goes like this: "I honestly thought God wouldn't let me get pregnant. I've always been a good Christian." And when magical thinking like that prevails, every time these girls do have sex without "getting caught," they only feel more and more invincible, safe from life's practical jokes to which the rest of us are subject. Safe, that is, until the one time the magic wears off.

"Teenagers think it's other people who have to die," says Bob Iles. "They are immortal. They think they can drive their cars a hundred miles an hour and there will be no accident. They can screw around in school, and when report-card time comes, make out just fine. They can have all the fun they want with their boyfriends on Saturday night and not get pregnant."

The fact that many sexually active girls still carry with them the message that sex is wrong is of no little consequence when it comes to contraceptive use — or the absence of it. By engaging in sex without planning far enough ahead to provide protection, some of the onus of guilt is lifted. And, way deep down, some may even feel that pregnancy would be a fitting punishment for their crimes of passion.

"Their reluctance to use birth control reflects these girls' moral ambivalence about whether it's acceptable to have sex at all," says Golden. "So they make a short-term decision to have sex when a long-term decision about birth control is too confining and too confusing."

Girls believe that birth control is not "natural," that it sullies the notion of "pure" love. "The idea that, in order to be natural, a sexual encounter must be accidental is tremendously destructive," says Peggy Golden. "Incidentally, they get that idea from us — their parents and from the rest of society. We love the 'ships passing in the night' fantasy."

Therefore, "good girls" may get caught up in the moment, but they certainly don't plan for it. They would not be found plunking down foam or jelly or a box of condoms on the drugstore counter along with their lipstick and mascara. That is a bold-faced admission to the world — and to themselves — that they plan to have sex.

And planning, to them, equals promiscuity.

Perhaps the most frightening explanation of all why

some teenage girls don't seem to be interested in protection is that, consciously or not, they want to have babies. In part, that may be because there is no longer the same awful social stigma attached to out-of-wedlock pregnancy there was just a few years back and, as we shall see, because a baby provides a purpose in life and someone to love. "Having a baby is not that uncool," said one cool, pregnant cucumber.

In sum, a variety of studies have found that adolescents who don't use contraceptives, or use them without conviction or consistency, do feel powerless and controlled by forces outside of themselves. Life seems to act *on* them, and they rarely feel competent to respond to its demands. Teens who shy away from birth control also tend to deny they are becoming sexual adults, and find it difficult to see how an action they take today may have a consequence tomorrow, while girls who are efficient contraceptors tend to accept themselves as more fully responsible, responsive sexual human beings.

And what of these girls' partners? While it is usually the girl and her family (or, through welfare payments, the rest of society) who pay the doctor bills and the diaper bills and all of the other costs of too-early pregnancy and motherhood, how much responsibility do boys feel toward the girls with whom they have sex?

According to the experts and to teenage girls (the real experts), most boys still aren't much interested in contraception. In a Planned Parenthood survey of 1,000 boys in the Chicago area, 43 percent said birth control was the girl's responsibility, while in a New York study boys cited as their primary reason for not using birth control that it interfered with their pleasure.

"Many boys still think that since it's the girl who gets

pregnant, it's the girl who should take responsibility for preventing the pregnancy," says Maurie Cullen. "But, lately, I've seen quite a few boys who are beginning to say, 'We need to do something, too.' "

(However, with all of the new methods available, it may now actually be more difficult to get boys to take responsibility than it was a generation ago, because then condoms were just about the only game in town, especially before the age of the free-and-confidential birth control clinics.)

Most girls don't give boys a very high contraception responsibility quotient. "Some guys say, 'I can't have sex with you if I have to use protection,' " claims a fifteen-year-old girl. "And it's sad how many girls fall for it."

Says another girl: "Boys either assume you've taken care of yourself or they don't think about it. Sometimes, two weeks or two months later, they remember to ask if you were safe. But they don't want to worry about it at the time."

Certainly, the media have always pretended males have nothing to do with contraception (except for the few condom ads in men's magazines that stress their pleasure properties over their protective qualities).

But perhaps things *are* changing, at least a bit: a 1978 Gallup Youth Survey shows that girls and boys, in almost equal numbers, want to be able to obtain contraceptives. And some girls do report sharing responsibility with their boyfriends. "Sam uses a rubber," reports Linda Frazier. "We asked ourselves, what would be easier? My mother couldn't take the Pill, and she and I are a lot alike, so I didn't want to try it, Other methods had disadvantages for us, too. So Sam said, 'I'll make it easy and take care of it.' I consider myself really lucky to have him."

And a sixteen-year-old boy whose girlfriend had a pregnancy scare: "Girls aren't the only ones who worry about pregnancies. They can wreck our lives, too. But I think a lot of us don't do much until our partners get pregnant."

While polls show that a healthy percentage of adults believe teenagers should be able to get birth control, those who are against it feel its availability would turn children into sexual addicts. But not a single study has given credence to that conjecture. On the other hand, slapping a prohibition on the distribution of contraception would not stop many kids from having sex.

Rose deSica found that out in a most painful way. When she found birth control pills in her daughter Angela's drawer (she said was looking for a scarf to borrow), Rose felt so angry and betrayed that she simply flushed the pills down the toilet without a word to her daughter.

Two months later, Angela was pregnant. The pregnancy was not her mother's fault, but Rose did overstep her bounds when she tried to make such an arbitrary choice for her daughter. When her mother found the pills, Angela had not yet had sex, but feeling angry and belittled by her mother's peremptory action, she proceeded to have intercourse without taking precautions.

"If we want to have sex, we will, regardless of whether birth control is there," says one girl. "Contraception doesn't lead to more sex, only to more responsible sex."

"If I am going to take on the responsibility of intercourse, then I also have to take on the responsibility of protecting myself," said Tricia, sixteen. "John and I talked about this from the beginning. We were already too scared about sex itself to add the fear of having a baby to the experience. So I got a diaphragm at a birth control clinic, and John also wears a rubber. They can be a hassle, but it's better than the fear."

Even though too few teenagers make use of birth control, and pregnancies are still too many, experts point out that contraception, when used with conviction and consistency, does work to keep the teen abortion rates way down. A 1978 Johns Hopkins study, conducted by Drs. Zelnick and Kantner, found that a probable 680,000 teenage pregnancies are avoided each year because teens do use birth control.

When it comes to making decisions about procreation, the Supreme Court decreed in 1977 that teenagers have the same rights as any other citizens, and that any restrictions on the distribution of contraceptives to minors is unconstitutional. Before, in many states, doctors were either obligated to inform parents or they could use their discretion when it came to telling parents that their children were seeking contraception.

So teens now have the legal right to obtain birth control through agencies funded by governmental monies without parents' knowledge or consent, although private doctors can — and some still do — choose to withhold birth control from adolescents.

Drs. Zelnick and Kantner, who are recognized specialists on teenage fertility and contraception, urge making birth control still more accessible to adolescents. "This would require increased availability through clinics, physicians, and drugstores, as well, perhaps, as through nonthreatening neighborhood-based peer networks — especially for distribution of nonphysician methods like condoms and foam," they write in the June 1978 issue of *Family Planning Perspectives*.

And, as the American College of Obstetricians and Gynecologists proclaimed several years ago: ". . . all barriers [to receiving contraception] should be removed even in the case of an unemancipated minor who refuses to involve her parents. A pregnancy should not be the price she has to pay for contraception. On the other hand, in counseling the patient, all possible efforts should be made to involve the parents."

Are most parents involved in these decisions? Do they want to be? Should they be? A 1978 Alan Guttmacher Institute study found that of the 1,450 girls surveyed in 10 states who get contraceptives from clinics, more than half *do* tell their parents. The other side of that statistic means that almost half leave their parents in the dark. And, according to a Nassau County, New York family-planning social worker, most parents whose children use birth control are not aware of it.

"But then it could be that some parents just don't want to admit to themselves that their kids are having sex and using birth control," says the social worker. "So we can't really know how many would object to our service if they 'knew,' or how many are actually saying to themselves, 'Thank goodness, she's taking care of herself and leaving us out of it.' "

Many parents who suspect their daughters are sexually active or are thinking of becoming so find themselves in a moral bind: does providing them with birth control imply an endorsement of sex? That certainly does not have to be a given. One mother shared with me what she told her daughter: "I'd rather you didn't have sex now, but if you choose to, I would hope you are protecting yourself. And if I can help you do that, I will." That is quite different from the mother who, wanting not to seem old-fashioned, or panicky at what her daughter might do without her intervention, practically pushes birth control on her daughter.

"Some parents prod their kids to be 'socially active,' " says Dr. Gary Strokosh. "They get a vicarious kick out of their kids' popularity, although they don't really want to know the details of that 'popularity.' While some of them will never bring up the subject of birth control, because they don't want to admit their daughters may be having sex, others shove birth control on their daughters and then carefully avoid the moral issues around it."

Another psychiatrist believes that mothers should never take their daughters by the hand to see the gynecologist, because such oversolicitousness implies they think of their daughters as children who can't make decisions for themselves. They may even end up encouraging their daughters, in defiance, to take "adult" actions — like having sex — before they are ready. Young women, he says, should always go to the doctor of their own accord, when the time is right for them.

Maurie Cullen agrees that the answer to the whole dilemma does not include unobtrusively slipping a six-months' supply of oral contraceptives under your daughter's pillow or presenting her with a gift certificate to the local gynecologist. "I know mothers who have said to their daughters, 'Well, you're thirteen now. I think it's time we went to the doctor and had you fitted for a diaphragm.' For that thirteen-year-old, that may be the last thing on her mind. Only when a girl shows some curiosity should a mother go about finding what her daughter's needs are."

But then what *does* a mother do? Can she, at least, offer to make an appointment for her daughter with her gynecologist? Or should she help her find her own doctor so the younger woman can feel secure that Mom can't intrude on the doctor-patient relationship? Is it really prying *that much* to ask if she needs birth control — or is going to need it soon?

Before we can answer those questions, we need to ask

ourselves other questions. Such as: Are we at least as interested in wanting to know what she is "up to" (which is another way of asking ourselves, when we aren't so sure, "Am I doing OK as a mother?") as we are in her contraceptive welfare? That is a very common concern, but one that is important to understand before we go barging into our daughter's life.

Do you know her well enough to trust that, if she is having sex, she can take the best — for her — measures to make sure she is not bringing a life into the world which neither of you is ready to nurture? If you aren't sure, the first question to ask her is not "Are you having sex?" or even "Are you using birth control?" but to ask *yourself,* "What information on birth control do I need, for myself and for my daughter?" And then set about to get that information, by going to the library or the bookstore, or sending for government pamphlets (your librarian has information on how to get those), or talking to your friends about their experience with various forms of birth control.

You can then make this information available to your daughter without prying into what she intends to do with it. One mother told me she said to her daughter, "Since you have begun dating, my own interest in sex and birth control has been piqued. I have gathered a lot of information about contraception, and I'd like you to have it too. When and whether you use that information is up to you — though do know I'm here for you if you want to talk."

While this chapter is not intended to include a definitive explanation of the merits or demerits of specific birth control techniques, it might be helpful to take a brief look at the methods teenagers are using.

We might as well start out with this not very encouraging word from Bob Iles: "There *are* no good birth control techniques for teenagers. Some have special physical risks for women who have not yet had children or whose hormonal systems are still in flux. Some just aren't practical for the many teenagers who only engage in occasional sex. Others are too much of a hassle for teens who don't want the bother."

According to the 1978 Johns Hopkins study cited earlier, a third of contraceptive-using teens reported using the Pill or IUD at last intercourse. When taken faithfully, oral contraceptives are reportedly 98.5 percent effective. While the rate of serious physical problems like thromboembolisms and tumors, very low in women of any age, are much lower in younger women, teens should be aware that oral contraceptives do carry some risks (which, as already stated, are less than are involved in carrying a child to term). However, some doctors don't like to prescribe birth control pills for a girl whose menstrual cycle is still irregular, nor do they think a daily dose of a medication taken internally is the best idea for a girl whose sex life is probably sporadic.

The new intrauterine devices like the Copper-7 are more effective than the older models for young women who have not yet borne a child. Side effects — sometimes attributed to IUD's — such as heavier menstrual periods and uterine infections are rare, but they do occur. And IUD's are reported to be almost as effective as the Pill in preventing pregnancy.

Many girls are becoming more interested in that old standby, the diaphragm, because of the drawbacks and hazards attributed to the Pill and the IUD. And when used regularly with vaginal foams or jellies, the diaphragm has almost the same effectiveness.

The most widely used nonmedical method of contraception is still the condom, even though many teens of both sexes claim not to like it very much. But when used consistently, in tandem with cream or foam (which are too messy and unromantic for many teens), effectiveness is high. All of these over-the-counter methods are relatively inexpensive and don't tamper with a girl's hormones or involve the constant presence of a foreign object in her body. But they do require mutual cooperation between partners — something many teenagers are not yet high on.

And contrary to evidence presented on *American Bandstand,* teenagers don't have a lot of rhythm, at least when it comes to birth control. As pointed out earlier, many girls have a tough time predicting their "safe periods," especially because the first few years after menses begin, periods are often irregular, making it difficult to predict the exact time of ovulation.

Then, of course, there is the still popular "withdrawal" method — which works about as well with today's teens as it always has worked.

In the next chapter, we will look at the consequences when the barriers to pregnancy and premature pregnancy fail or are simply ignored. And those consequences are frightening.

# 8

## *To Be or Not To Be a Mother at Fifteen*

"Human beings are not designed, either in body or spirit, for the experience of adolescent pregnancy."

— *Melvin Konner, medical biologist, Harvard University*

"The girl who has an illegitimate child at the age of 16 suddenly has 90 per cent of her life's script written for her. Her life choices are few, and most of them are bad.

—*Arthur Campbell, director, The Population Institute*

AND YET, IN A TIME IN HISTORY when women have more "life choices" than ever before — good ones, we've heard, when contraception is more accessible and pregnancy rates among all other age groups have dropped almost 30 percent — each year more than 600,000 girls under eighteen — the number who are having babies — are opting for a "life script," as we shall see, with a predictable three-handkerchief ending. (A million girls are actually getting pregnant every year.)

However you balance the figures, the problem of teenage pregnancy and motherhood is staggering. One out of every 10 girls will become pregnant this year. Nearly 3 in 10 sexually active teenagers will eventually be pregnant. The birthrate among girls in this country is 12 times higher than it is in Japan, and significantly higher than in many so-called underdeveloped nations.

The most alarming increase is occurring among girls under fifteen — a 75 percent jump during the early seventies, according to Planned Parenthood data, which also stated that, in a recent year, 3,000 thirteen-year-olds actually became mothers. And belying that old saw about those who are burned once tending to shy away from the flame, 60 percent of the girls who have a baby before they blow out the candles on their sixteenth birthday cake will become pregnant again by the time they are eighteen.

The risks — physical, psychological, and social — of pregnancy and childbirth are much greater for an adolescent and her child. A 1976 federal government study has said that pregnant teenagers have a 30 percent higher death rate in childbirth, a 30 percent higher infant mortality rate, a 15 percent rate of miscarriage, and a 36 percent higher rate of premature birth than do women in the next higher age group.

In turn, prematurity and low birth weight increase infants' chances of epilepsy, cerebral palsy, and mental retardation. Teenage mothers-to-be are also more likely to suffer complications like toxemia, anemia, bleeding during pregnancy, and prolonged labor.

What are some of the social penalities paid by young mothers? Eight of 10 women who become mothers at seventeen or younger don't complete high school. Often, they face a long and permanent ride on the welfare rolls; almost $5 billion in federal funds go to teenage mothers and their children each year — three-fourths get some kind of public aid.

Of those who marry the fathers of their children, around three-quarters will be divorced within five years. The statistics also say that a woman who had a baby as a teenager has less of a chance of ever making a marriage work than does the "average" woman.

There are other less tangible, but no less painful results. "Premature motherhood cuts short the daydreaming that is such a fundamentally important part of being an adolescent," says Jacquie Ficht, a nurse practitioner who counsels teenagers. "This daydreaming — which can drive parents crazy — is the means by which they begin to find their place in the world and in the universe, whereas until now they only dealt with their place in the family.

"For when you are fifteen years old and up at two A.M. every night with a baby who's screaming bloody murder, and you are exhausted the rest of the time, all the daydreaming and looking ahead is cut off. Your place in the world, in the future, suddenly seems to be set in concrete."

And yet it is the children of these confused, ambivalent young mothers who may ultimately pay the highest price. "The offspring of adolescent mothers are more likely to have impaired intellectual functioning," says Melvin Konner of Harvard University. "Poverty, divorce, inept parenting, child neglect and child abuse are all more frequent in their homes. These children often grow up to be angry, destructive people, unable to form living, human attachments, and destined to repeat the cycle of early childbearing and early marriage — with more failure at both."

But it is not only the sheer numbers of girls who are becoming pregnant, nor the consequences that follow that are capturing headlines. Rather, what is grabbing attention is *who* is now being caught in the act. When the only girls who seemed to be getting pregnant were poor ghetto dwellers, no one got very excited. Now teenage pregnancy is a social disease to which white, advantaged middle-class girls — the same girls who are being assured that the best and the brightest is theirs — seem to be most susceptible.

Aside from social class, a composite portrait of the girl most at risk for pregnancy, drawn from a number of researchers, includes these characteristics: her relationship with her parents often lacks give-and-take openness; divorce and divisiveness are common in her family; her father is frequently absent.

She is often lonely, depressed, and passive and thinks she is "bad." School may be a problem, as is her view of herself as a sexual being. And she is no more sexually active than her peers.

"They are actually a very sexually conservative group of girls," says Linda Lowrey, a nurse practitioner who works with pregnant teenagers. "They probably masturbate less frequently than other girls, and, if you ask them, you will find quite a few who don't even condone premarital sex."

In sum, as one researcher points out: "The pregnant teenager is a girl with a syndrome of failure — failure to fulfill her adolescent functions — to remain in school, limit her family, establish stable values, be self-supporting, and have healthy infants."

The question I keep coming back to, in different forms and shadings: What is the meaning of the upsurge in pregnancies in a time and place where girls have been promised so many opportunities to be whoever or whatever they want to be? Shouldn't too-early pregnancy be part of the old game, the preliberation mind-set?

And as I have said before, the new sex role–less opportunities are still opportunities without definition, without precedent, without role models who have walked the freedom road before. Early motherhood saves these girls from the unknown. And while inflation and recession are very real bogeypersons, the position of mother is always open, no training or prior experience required.

Having a baby can be an excellent defense against competing for the goodies the world promises. Girls see that training for a job guarantees nothing. They may not see much evidence in their parents' lives that working and waiting for the good life pays off, or that playing by the rules means you will win. Not to mention that the rules themselves seem more and more vague.

Despite all the promised-land rhetoric, many teenagers don't see the options open to them as real and are diving back into traditional waters. A baby may give them a purpose, a sense of self, a little dignity and respect — or so they think. It is something to *do*; it is something even *they* can accomplish. And a baby also provides someone over whom a young girl can exercise power when everyone else seems to hold sway over her.

"So many girls don't see how they can have an effect on the world in which they live," says psychologist Judith Stevens-Long. "The problems we face as a nation, as a world, seem insoluble. Having a baby is an attempt to make it all have meaning."

As if in agreement, a young woman of sixteen years and a mouthful of braces says: "My school counselor says all the tests showed I was so good at math, I could be an engineer. But no one in my family has finished college, and it scares me. So now I'm pregnant and it doesn't much matter. I'll be a good mother. I'm just not sure of the other stuff."

As clinical psychologist Rita Blau says, pregnancy can be an attempt to establish a degree of (pseudo?) independence while avoiding venturing out into the world. "Of the pregnant girls I studied, the predominant attitude may not have been 'women's place is in the home,' but it was, at least, 'it is safer and more predictable within these four walls.' "

So pregnancy, while seeming to confer instant adulthood, really allows a leap back to childhood by bringing mother and daughter back together, often in an unspoken pact of interdependence.

These young pregnancies are definitely creating a new class of dependent women, dependent on men, dependent on the welfare system, and dependent on their mothers, if not physically or financially, then psychically. The apron strings are kept securely tied; only the appearance is loosened. For to go out in the world means they would have to accomplish something apart from Mother, and that is something many of them are not prepared to do.

Experts also tell us that more teenagers are getting pregnant and carrying their pregnancies to fruition because the whole enterprise carries with it far less stigma than it did only a decade or so earlier. As Jacqueline Ficht puts it: "If you or I had become pregnant at fifteen, we would have been shipped off to Aunt Clara in Wisconsin, and when we came back we would have pleaded a nine-month case of mononucleosis that required country food and rest. Today, thanks to the media's glorification of rock and movie stars who advertise their out-of-wedlock pregnancies, it is okay to be an unwed mother.

"The difference is that most girls don't have the support systems available to your 'average' rock star."

And while it is undeniably good that early pregnancy and motherhood no longer automatically confer the Mark of Cain on the perpetrators and their unfortunate progeny, how sad if so many of our young women are taking this as license to have children before they are ready.

License is not liberation.

Girls are also opting for a career of premature motherhood for another, very disturbing reason. While theoretically adults have babies in order to give love, express caring, and nurture a new life, teenagers often have babies to create a ready-made someone to love them.

"Girls tell me they want to love and take care of a baby," says Maurie Cullen, "but I know that that's a projection of the caring and the unconditional acceptance they want for themselves."

Tina, sixteen, quiet and sweet, is an otherwise intelligent girl who thinks that a baby would fill the gaps in her life. "I'd like to have something I could be completely responsible for and sacrifice everything for, because nothing else is important in my life right now," she says. "It would be neat, I think, to have someone like a baby who is completely dependent on me."

Tina, it is clear, has a yawning emotional void in her life. She needs to know that she is valued, loved, that she can get the emotional nourishment she needs. But she won't get that from a helpless infant who needs those things from her. She has fantasies that if someone would "sacrifice everything" for her, then *she* would be worth something.

The loneliness and depression of these girls may run very deep, and to the teenager for whom "now" is forever, the pain appears to be without end. A baby, she figures, may be just the thing to turn the tide; after all, no one or nothing else has been able to.

"In my fantasy, if I got pregnant, I would go to a home for unwed mothers and everyone would be really warm and caring and I would have my baby there," said a young girl who has flirted with pregnancy a number of times. "In fact, I've gone so far as to find out where five of those homes are. I have the whole nine months planned out."

A girl may become pregnant — or anorexic, or suicidal, or may experiment with drugs — says Virginia Satir, "when she can no longer project, rationalize, or ignore her pain. The only avenue left seems to be escape, and pregnancy becomes a means to freedom."

"My parents scream and yell at me all the time. I can't take it much longer. If I had a kid, I wouldn't have my parents standing over me, telling me what to do. Though I guess the welfare department might."

Pregnancy can also be a cry for attention. "A lot of girls get pregnant when their parents are so involved with their own lives they barely notice them," says high school counselor Karen Speros. "Some of the girls get pregnant twice — or more — if the first time doesn't get them the attention they need."

"You see, this baby is *mine*," explains Marie as she points to a tiny, sleeping bundle. "My parents had always given me lots of *things*, but nothing I felt was mine. I was living in their house, eating their food, but they were so busy that even the time they could spare me felt like it was borrowed. It seemed as if everything I had was on loan from them.

"I didn't get pregnant on purpose — at least not that I'm aware of — but I didn't even consider an abortion or giving my baby up for adoption. My parents wanted me to; they kept screaming about how I would ruin their lives. You see how everything was always done for their convenience? Even my being there was an inconvenience.

"I swear I'll never let my little girl feel like that."

Some girls become pregnant as an unconscious attempt to smooth over a troubled relationship with their mothers, or to make an angry statement about the mothering they have received, or even to prove to themselves and their mothers that they can succeed at mothering where their own mothers failed.

"I would like a daughter so I could teach her to love herself," says a fifteen-year-old who takes only cursory precautions against pregnancy. "My mother didn't do that for me. I know I would get attached to my kid, but I'm sure *I* would know when she needs more space of her own. My mother just won't let go at all."

It is *not* uncommon for a strained relationship to improve when a daughter gets pregnant; often, mothers and daughters become partners in shared misery. And, for the first time, a mother may confess to her pregnant daughter that she, too, had an unwanted pregnancy. (These girls are very often the daughters of women who themselves had very young premarital pregnancies.) So they can now identify with one another.

"Where there may have been horrendous discord before, there is now a resolution of sorts. 'What's done is done,'" says Maurie Cullen. "There is a pulling together over a mutual concern. 'What will *we* do now?' 'How can *I* help her?'"

Virginia Satir points out that in families where a woman's whole life is invested in her role as mother, her daughter's pregnancy can be a form of self-validation. "Existentially, she is confirmed because her daughter is following in her footsteps. Also, she may have desperately wanted another child of her own but didn't, for any number of reasons, have one.

"Her daughter has gotten a filtered message and is subconsciously fulfilling her mother's need for a new child and her own need to please her mother."

The mother, on one level angry that her daughter has done a "stupid" thing, is, on another level, pleased.

Of course, most parents are deeply anguished about their daughters' pregnancies.

"When Wendy told me she was pregnant, my first reaction was anger. When I cooled off, I knew I was scared for her and disappointed in both of us. It was like all the years I had tried to be a good mother had come down to this moment, and I wasn't sure whether I had failed her or she had failed me."

Janine Siegel is a good woman, a good mother, who never thought anything like this could happen to her. "Both of us went to a counselor and became convinced that, for Wendy, abortion was probably the best answer. She wasn't ready to be a mother yet, and though she thinks she loves the father of her child, she certainly wasn't prepared to be a wife.

"I had just gone back to school to get the teaching credential I had put aside years ago, and I wasn't ready to give that up again to mother Wendy's child. But the decision was never easy.

"We both had a tremendous sense of loss. Wendy was losing a child she wasn't entirely sure she wanted to give up. Becoming pregnant also signaled to her the loss of her own childhood, and she saw that even though she had made the decision to become actively sexual, she was afraid to grow up. She realized she had tried to do it too early, and she was guilty that her sexuality — with which she was not altogether comfortable — had culminated to this.

"My initial anger, I came to understand, was partly because I had lost my self-image as the perfect mother whose kid could do no wrong. I was also losing the ideas I cherished of my daughter as my little girl. And, of course, I was losing my grandchild."

Janine Siegel is obviously still shaken by the experience. "Abortion is never easy for anyone involved. There is nothing clean-cut about the decision. No one who has been personally involved can say with real conviction that they are 'for it' or 'against it.'

"But, in our case, it seemed like the best decision we could make, given the almost unbearably difficult circumstances."

The counseling Wendy and her mother received, both before and after the abortion, was crucial for their growth and their understanding of the meaning of the pregnancy. And understanding the meaning of a phenomenon is the only thing that can keep us from repeating it.

Let's look at the option the Siegels chose — abortion.

Even though more girls are choosing to have and to keep their babies, these days, about 27 percent of pregnancies to fifteen-to-nineteen-year-olds are terminated by abortion, as are 45 percent of pregnancies to girls under fifteen, according to a 1977 study from the Alan Guttmacher Institute. Teenagers obtain one-third of all abortions in the country. By the time they leave their teens, 13 percent of today's young women will have had an abortion.

Whatever our own moral or ethical considerations, a special HEW task force on teenage pregnancy reported in 1979 that abortions are "essential to reduce the numbers of high risk adolescent births." Though assigned to find alternatives to abortion, the panel reported that the only alternatives to abortion they could come up with were "suicide, motherhood and, some would add, madness."

The panel concluded: "Even if funding is not available

for pregnancy termination, we recommended that health and service providers make available abortion information and counseling and, where appropriate, referrals to abortion services, to permit the adolescent a full range of choices and to assist those who do choose to terminate their pregnancy to receive adequate and safe abortion services."

Free access to information and counseling on all the alternatives also seems essential to avoid future unplanned, unwanted pregnancies.

"When a pregnant girl comes to our clinic, it is very important she knows she has a free choice about having an abortion, continuing the pregnancy and keeping the baby, or putting the baby up for adoption," says Linda Lowrey. "If she feels that someone else made the decision for her to have an abortion, we will see her back in three to six months, pregnant again."

In general, studies have found that teenagers who choose abortion are more likely to have higher educational and career aspirations, to come from middle-class or higher backgrounds, to value control over their own lives, to see themselves as competent, to do better in school, and to be less traditional when it comes to sex-role attitudes than are girls who choose to continue their pregnancies.

On the other hand, girls who choose to have and keep their babies — and more than three of four who give birth are now keeping them — are more impulsive, less calm, less financially and socially well-off, and are more often uncomfortable discussing sex with their parents.

In fact, some of these girls would sooner have their babies than either discuss their situation with parents or other adults who might be able to help, or think about the lifelong problems that only begin with becoming an underage mother.

And aside from all the other reasons girls are having babies, there is a strange new pressure — both from within themselves and from their peers — for pregnant girls to "pay the piper" and thus keep their babies. "These teenagers are very moral, and they believe they should ante up for their mistakes," says Linda Lowrey. "Since they generally don't feel that having sex in the first place was acceptable, getting pregnant and raising the baby may be a fitting punishment."

Says seventeen-year-old Bonnie: "I was dumb enough to get this way" — she points an accusing finger at her billowing midsection — "and I should have to go all the way with it."

As already mentioned, teenage mothers often have come into the world themselves the product of such a decision. "They may keep their babies out of a sense of gratitude to their own mothers," says Karen Speros. "It's a strange sort of Catch-22 predicament, because while their mothers don't want to express regret over the existence of any of their children, many would like to advise their daughters to postpone having children.

"But how can you recommend your daughter have an abortion without sounding as if your life would have been better had *you* aborted *her*?"

What can be done to stem the tide of teenage pregnancies? On an organizational level, schools could train counselors to be aware of the girls most at-risk for pregnancy and attempt to reach out to them. Neighborhood, peer-based birth control distribution programs or mass-media approaches in which teenage heroes talk of responsibility and respect and sex could help. More information about the realities of parenting might open some eyes, while the best pregnancy prevention programs would un-

doubtably be those that seek to strengthen family ties —
but then, that is easier said than done.

For those girls who will become and have become
mothers, there are good programs across the country which
help them handle pre- and postnatal care, teach them to
accept responsibility as parents, and help them to finish
school and learn a trade. You can find out about them by
contacting local mental health agencies or medical centers
that have programs for adolescents.

How can *we* help our daughters delay the start of their
mothering careers?

We need to know that a young pregnancy is often preceded by a crisis such as the death of a parent or a friend,
parents' divorce, the pregnancy of a friend, being uprooted
to a new town, being cast off by a boyfriend. If there has
recently been such a crisis in your daughter's life, it might
be a good idea to pay special attention to her, making sure
she knows she is loved and that, in whatever changing
forms, the family will pull out of its problems.

And no family is without problems; neither is there
such an animal as a perfect parent. But, as I have said before, it is so important not to pretend problems don't exist.
Our daughters need to feel included in the whole of our
lives — including, on occasion, the places where it hurts.
And the odds are that they will be much less likely to turn
elsewhere — like the arms of a boy or the imagined promises of a baby — for emotional succor.

Just as you share with your daughter information about
contraception and the emotional consequences of very early
sexual activity, so too can you share what you have learned
about the risks to health and to emotional and financial
security posed by very early pregnancy. Again, the idea is
not to lecture or to frighten her, but to help her see what is

wise so she can choose what will really work for her at this point in her life.

The National Organization for Non-Parents, a group that advocates informed parenthood, has published a list of questions to help individuals of any age to decide whether to be or not to be a parent. Though these questions are addressed to anyone who is thinking about having a child, it might be very helpful for you and your daughter to consider and discuss the following questions.

What do I want out of life for myself? Do I have the time and energy to handle a child and a job (and school)? Am I ready to give up the freedom to do what I want, when I want to do it?

Can I afford to support a child? Do I even know how much it takes to raise a child? How would a child interfere with *my* growth and development and future educational plans?

Do I like doing things with children? Would I put pressure on a child to achieve things I hadn't? Do I expect my child to make my life happy? Would I take things out on a child if I lost my temper? How do I get along with my own parents? What if I have a child and find out I made a wrong decision?

Do I believe having a child would show others how mature I am? Do my partner and I understand each other's feelings about religion, work, family, child raising, future goals? Will children fit in with these feelings, hopes, and plans?

Other questions you might reflect on together: If necessary, am I equipped to be the main source of emotional sustenance for my baby? How much help do I expect of my own mother? Am I ready to marry? Am I prepared to tell my dates that I can't stay out late because I must be up early with my little one? And, even though our morals appear to be changing, am I ready to face the disapproval of others?

These questions can be enlightening for you, as the parent of a teenager, to meditate on. Are they questions you considered before *you* took the leap into parenthood? Would your life, or the lives of your children, have been altered in any way if you had?

Have you been resentful of your daughter because you were not as thoughtful before she was conceived? Can you discuss with her your thoughts about what it has meant to you to have her in your life?

And how about your feelings about becoming a grandmother at forty? You're still young, just beginning to see the light at the end of the tunnel of responsibility for your own children. You may be planning to get a job or start a new career, to go back to school, or just begin thinking about your own needs first. Becoming a grandmother right now — especially when that may mean assuming at least part of the responsibility for the new mother and child — is probably not your idea of a fantasy come true.

If your daughter is pregnant or already has a child and if you are to be able to help her at all, it is important that you face your own considerations, embarrassment, anger, and disappointment, Do some reflecting and see if at least some of your concern can be summed up in thoughts like: Why is she doing this to *me*? What did *I* do to deserve this? Was I such a bad parent? What will my friends (our minister, my mother-in-law, et cetera) think of me now?

You aren't bad or crazy or even different from almost anyone else for having thoughts like those. Many of us tend to take nearly everything personally, as if life does what it does with our pain and pleasure specifically in mind. In reality, life is too busy simply unfolding to notice whether we like it or not.

But it is necessary, not only for our own aliveness, but for our daughters', if we refuse to be run by our anxieties. We must look past what our feelings seem to be telling us, and see what the thoughts are behind the feelings. Embarrassment may mean we are overly concerned with how we look to others. Disappointment can indicate that *we* feel responsible (actually, to blame) for all that happens in our lives and the lives of those we care about. Anger often pops up when we are afraid of losing something, and here we might be fearful of losing our image of the person we want to think we are — a good mother who has done a good job.

If your daughter can see clarity in you — or at least see that you are *interested* in seeing clearly — she can begin to sort out what is most intelligent for herself.

And if she is pregnant it would be easy now — too easy — for the whole family to focus its attention on her and silently believe she is, if not accuse her outright of being, "what is wrong" with the family system. So it's very important for everyone to look at what ideas have been important to the status and the status quo of the family that have now manifested themselves in her pregnancy. What family fears or fantasies did she pick up? Do only grand gestures rally the family together in a positive or even an angry way? (To our egos, attention is attention, good or bad.) Do *you* cherish very young children more than you do older kids, so that bringing a new babe into the world might be a way for her to get more love, even love once removed?

Again, the answers to these questions should not be an occasion for guilt, but only for the understanding which leads to growth.

Following is a list of agencies and organizations that can provide more information and assistance:

• The National Foundation–March of Dimes, 1275 Mamaroneck Avenue, White Plains, NY 10605 (or your local chapter of March of Dimes), for information on parenting–education programs in your area.

• Family Learning Center, New Brunswick Public Schools, 225 Comstock Street, New Brunswick, NJ 08902. Materials and information on education programs for school-age parents.

• Education for Parenthood Program. National Center for Child Advocacy, Children's Bureau, Administration for Children, Youth and Families, P.O. Box 1182, Washington, D.C. 20013, for information on a program to help teenagers prepare for effective parenthood through working with young children and learning about child development and the role of parents. The program is offered through school systems and voluntary organizations to help improve the competence of teenagers as parents, in the recognition that several hundred thousand are becoming parents each year. If the course is not offered in your area, you can find out how to initiate it.

• Executive Deputy Commission of Education, U.S. Office of Education, Washington, D.C. Illustrative program materials and summary of commercially developed parenting education materials.

• Parents' Magazine Films, Inc., 52 Vanderbilt Ave., New York, NY 10017. Audiovisual programs on marriage, parenthood, child behavior, development and health, pregnancy and prenatal care, and family living. Write for information and descriptive brochures.

Having a baby is one way a young woman can try to back out of the obligations that seem to have become a part of being a citizen of these boastfully liberated times.

It is obviously an extreme measure. There are other measures — some more extreme, even final — that girls are using to try to tell us that they simply cannot squeeze themselves into a specific, demanding mold that can fit no one individual with any accurate meaning or comfort.

Drugs and drinking are but another language girls have learned to voice their confusion and pain and unwillingness to be anyone other than who they are, as we shall see.

# 9

## *Drugs and Alcohol: Escape from Living through Chemistry*

SARAH BROOKS AND ANNIE CROCETTI, now respectively fifteen and seventeen, live in the same city, but so far on opposite sides of the track it is doubtful they will ever meet. While seeming to be total demographic opposites, they share a common problem that makes them sisters of a sort. Though Annie is a child of divorce and of subsequent downward mobility, and Sarah's parents are both busy and successful divorce lawyers who gave Sarah everything they were sure a child needed and would be grateful for, both girls have been heavily involved with drugs and/or alcohol.

Annie received her drug education in the streets, while Sarah's lessons were learned in a posh and private school for girls. ("Miss Something-or-Other's") in a much more fashionable enclave of the Los Angeles sprawl.

We'll return later to Sarah and Annie, for their experience tells us much about the drug problem among young women today.

By now it should come as no revelation to anyone that teenage drinking and drug abuse are major problems in this country, affecting families from every side of the social and economic fence. According to a 1977 Gallup Youth Survey, teenagers themselves consider the use and abuse of drugs and alcohol to be the biggest problem facing their generation.

While it is not my intent to overload you with a barrage of statistics, for a general overview of the problem, suffice it to say that while more young people smoke marijuana daily than take a drink every day, alcohol remains the number one adolescent drug problem. That is true in numbers of users and abusers, in dollars and cents, in disease and death and shattered lives and illusions. According to the Department of Health, Education and Welfare, 3.5 million teenagers have a drinking problem.

Over a third of teenagers have dabbled at one time or another in various outlaw drugs other than pot, including stimulants, tranquilizers, hallucinogens, such as LSD, THC, PCP, mescaline, and peyote, and cocaine and opiates.

But the newer wrinkle on the problem, as I mentioned earlier, is that "substance abuse," far from being the largely male problem it was not many years ago, is now hitting girls like Annie and Sarah at least as hard as it hits boys. You might even say — with more than a trace of rueful irony — that when it comes to drugs and alcohol and adolescence, the sexes are finally becoming equal. And in some respects, girls are even more equal than boys and getting equaler all the time.

Take alcohol. Only twenty years ago, boys who drank and got drunk outnumbered girls by a wide margin. Today, according to a number of surveys, girls drink as early as boys, as often, and "drink to get drunk" with the same frequency.

Girls are also giving boys a run for their drug money. According to the National Institute on Drug Abuse, while equal proportions of adolescent females and males are using drugs, they have developed different tastes. *More girls than boys use tranquilizers, and girls take stimulants more often than do boys, while boys still hold the edge when it comes to hallucinogens and cocaine.*

And even tobacco — the real devil weed — has become a serious problem for very young females. For while the Surgeon General reports that a large percentage of teenage boys have been liberated from smoking over the last twenty years, the number of teenage girls who have taken up the nicotine habit has actually increased eightfold. The experts say the increase is due to girls' feeling more postliberation stress and competition. Girls themselves add that they think smoking is "sexy," "cool," or "grown-up," apparently all states today's youngest women are aching to attain.

Which brings me back to "that" question (only the symptoms and semantics vary): What does this new sexual parity, in the matter of substance abuse, tell us about the state of being a young woman today?

To provide background for the answer to that question, let me point out that researchers — and casual observers — have long been aware that men often drink to feel "more like men" — that is, more assertive, uninhibited, powerful. Traditionally, because of different kinds of cultural expectations and experiences, it's also been duly noted that women frequently imbibe in order to "feel more like women" — which, at least in the past, has meant more affectionate, sexier, more open, and prettier.

Has liberation changed all that?

Psychologist John Bolf tells me that many of the young

men he treats in his substance abuse program are still trying to "fulfill their male identities" through drugs, while drug-using girls are now announcing their new freedom by getting high. "And it is also a way of saying that they just aren't happy in spite of that freedom," Bolf points out.

In addition, growing numbers of studies are showing that adult women are apparently turning to liquor more often these days because they are confused about what their roles are and insecure about the meaning of femininity and femaleness, and generally don't feel up to what the world expects of them. Apparently, as has been duly noted, the glittering expectations that women can and should make it in the heretofore male world are still light-years ahead of what many women — young and older — currently think they are up to.

As therapist Joyce Lindenbaum puts it, alcohol and drugs seem to be tranquilizing girls against the uncertainty of being female in the 1980s.

Studies have also found that today's teenage girls — much more so than boys — drink because they are afraid of *losing* something — a parent or a parent's love, another human being they hold dear, including a boyfriend, their looks, even their youth. And could it be possible that they are also frightened of losing the carefully manicured image of themselves as girls/women, which their foremothers clung to? No matter how limiting, it was known, and in familiarity may lie comfort, definition, security. The old order at least gave young women an idea of who they were and who they could go on to be.

Now that that structure is missing, drugs may render a substitute sense of definition. It has even been hypothesized that drugs and booze have replaced the now-obsolete rituals of growing up — the coming-out and the sweet-sixteen parties of the fifties and the sit-ins and marches of the Vietnam years — that helped to mark the passage from childhood to adulthood.

Apparently, drugs and booze are a rite on which a lot of young people are booking passage. "The kid who doesn't drink may feel like a square peg in a round hole," says Pat Mitchell, director of a drug abuse program for juveniles. "Teens judge themselves by other kids' outsides. When they have a couple of drinks, they think their outsides match with everybody else's."

Or as a seventeen-year-old says: "The more you drink, the more accepted you are. Everyone does it now, even the jocks and the cheerleaders. A lot of people can't have a good time unless they're stoned or drunk. And it's the only way some kids can take things in stride."

It was a very few years ago that drugs also represented a defiant nose thumbing toward the way things were or an attempt to transcend the boundaries laid down by that amorphous parent of us all, referred to as the Establishment.

"Today," says Shari Glucoft-Wong, "most kids who smoke dope do so to party, or just to get to sleep. They are more involved in their immediate lives and less so in the cosmos."

Or, as a Gallup Youth Survey indicates, young people today are less prone to point out the injustices of the world or to take action to obviate its pressures. Instead, they just want time out from them. Drugs provide that.

"There is a lot of pressure, especially now on girls, to do well in school and in life," says a would-be cheerleader, sixteen. "Kids are afraid they aren't going to graduate. They have a lot of family problems. They want to escape, but if they don't want to give up all the comforts of home, they just nod-out for a while. Your parents probably won't even notice you aren't really there."

In the case of Sarah Brooks, that was unfortunately true. Her parents love her very much — there never was any doubt about that, but for a while they were just too caught up in the busyness of their own lives to be able to see her.

By the time Sarah's parents did recognize she had a problem, Sarah was full-tilt into a terrifying roller-coaster ride of alcohol, marijuana, uppers and downers, cocaine, psychedelics, and more. And, as almost always happens, she took the rest of her family along for the ride. "I was stoned most of the time, before, during, and after school," says Sarah. "For a long time my parents couldn't tell I was out of it. My mom though my moods and lack of energy were from working so hard in my accelerated classes, which I had been doing until I just couldn't hack it anymore. I think I was into every kind of drug except heroin. After a while, I couldn't even remember what I was on at any one time."

"We all seemed to be falling apart," said Andrea Brooks. "My husband and I couldn't agree on how to handle Sarah and we fought a lot. Our younger son and daughter were having nightmares and were beginning to have trouble in school."

At first, her parents tried cutting off her allowance, hoping that things would be all right when Sarah had no money to buy drugs. But then she simply sold her own belongings, and then some of her mother's jewelry and her father's coin collection. Next, her parents tried talking to her, yelling at her, and screening her phone calls. Nothing seemed to work.

Finally, the Brookses found a drug rehabilitation center for teenagers, and though Sarah has been "clean" for several months now, she is still sometimes shaky. Her parents spend more time with all of their children and are careful to try not to push them into a particular mold. And they talk — and listen — to each other now.

"I was always the daughter of David and Andrea, star attorneys," explains Sarah. "When I got loaded, I was someone else — although I was never quite sure who. Now that I'm straight, I'm beginning to find out."

Annie Crocetti's life-style slipped a notch when her parents divorced, and along with it, so did her picture of herself.

"When I was in the sixth grade, my parents got divorced. After that, there was a lot less money, so my mom and I and my younger sisters had to move to a neighborhood I guess you would call lower-class, a lot of poor black and Chicano people.

"My mother got remarried pretty quick to this guy ten years younger than she is, and he was stoned all the time. He and I didn't get along. After that, nothing was the same. It seemed like there was no reason for me to stay the same either. So I started hanging out down at the beach, and I met a lot of rough people. Finally, I ran away and slept in abandoned houses and in parks and that kinda stuff. I was hiding from the police, from my parents, and from myself.

"I don't want to sound like Miss Innocent, but that was the first time I realized there was more to life than school and studying and playing dolls. I found out about the streets, and I found out about some heavy drinking and drugs. Mostly, I was into booze. I guess I have to say I was an alcoholic.

"I met a guy who was ten years older than me. He was heavy into drugs. We fell in love and were gonna run away, back to New York. I wanted to go back to where I was a kid. But the night before we were supposed to leave I got scared and called my father.

"Now I live with my father and my stepmother. We get along okay. You know what's sad, though? My mother married this young dude so she could feel younger, and I ran away and did dope and got involved with an older guy so I would feel older.

"It seems like nobody wants to be who they are anymore. Dope and booze and sex are ways to pretend that things are different."

Moving to a different neighborhood and into a more stable environment, along with regular visits to a counselor, helped Annie face her problems. She is now a B+ student looking forward to college.

How do Sarah and Annie fit into the demographic picture of the teenage drug and/or alcohol abuser? A Rutgers University study found that young abusers often are depressed and normless and have faltering opinions of their own worth. And, according to John Bolf, the worse a teen's self-esteem, the more likely she will be to sample a smorgasbord of drugs because she hopes that something will help.

Beside having sagging self-esteem, both Annie and Sarah were alienated from their families; it mattered little that the appearance of the alienation was different. Studies show that the kid who isn't close to her family is at much higher risk to have abuse problems and more likely to choose her friends from among other users.

Though we tend to believe that the big cities — particularly those at either end of the country — have the biggest drug problems, there is little variation in drug use between the South, East, West, or the heartlands, nor between urban or rural America. And any gaps there have been appear to be narrowing.

Generally, young people who plan to go to college use fewer drugs, except for marijuana, which is smoked with the same frequency by college- and noncollege-bound students. Drug users are also less likely to be involved in traditional religions. Of those who have a religious background, there are more Jewish and Catholic teenagers who dabble in drugs and drink, but more Protestants and Mormons who are abusers.

And while, economically, Sarah's family was much closer to the top of the heap, no socioeconomic stratum offers protection against the problem. It doesn't really matter whether Dad comes home and groans, "God, do I need a martini," or shouts, "Edith, where's my beer?" Or even if, in times of stress, Mom heads straight for the medicine chest to pop the prescription the doctor gave her to tide her through the rough times that eventually became a way of life. The message is the same: life is something to be coped with, and alcohol or pills have always seemed to be damned good coping mechanisms for everything from boredom to loneliness.

"Alcohol or Valium has always seemed to make life easier for Mom and Dad," says John Bolf, "so why shouldn't it work for the kids? Teenage alcoholism is as big a problem as it is because our society views drinking as a way to ease tension, an important component of all socializing, an acceptable solitary pastime, and a preferred substitute to drugs."

Many parents are actually relieved that their kids "only" take an occasional drink rather than a toke on a joint. It seems that when children turn to drugs, parents experience a rejection of their values. But drinking — after all, such a universal social behavior — is often seen as a step toward adulthood. Didn't we all get bombed a few times on our way out of adolescence — and after?

Some studies say that teens from families where one or both parents have an alcohol problem are more likely than the average to have drinking problems of their own. On the other hand, parents who preach total abstinence under penalty of hellfire also produce a higher-than-average percentage of alcoholic children.

We need to remember that adolescence is a time of experimentation and that drugs and alcohol are facts of your daughter's life today, so it isn't abnormal when a young woman tries pot or wants to see what getting drunk is all about. But *abuse*, while so frightfully common, shouldn't be accepted as the status quo. A healthy adolescent who gets a sense of who she is from within and from her relationships with those who truly value her may very well give marijuana or getting drunk a try or two and then forget about them. Reality itself becomes such a compelling place a teenager needs no long vacations into unreality.

Whether or not drugs or alcohol are problems in your family, there are a number of issues which you and your daughter might want to look at together. (And, like sex, it would be a mistake to assume, as some parents do, that there is no reason to discuss those issues because "*My* kid isn't involved. If she were, I'd know about it.") Who, for instance, chooses whether and when she can drink? Should she be allowed to go to parties where everyone knows liquor will be served? Should she be able to serve liquor — even beer — at her own parties in your home? Whose responsibility is it to see to the welfare of her guests if they drink too much? What does she do if she is with a date who becomes drunk or high? What does she do if she finds herself caring for a boy for whom getting stoned is important?

To help young people determine if they have a real drinking problem, Alcoholics Anonymous has prepared a list of questions. By changing a few key words, the list can also be used to look at whether drugs are a problem. According to A.A., a "yes" to one question is a warning; a "yes" to as few as three questions means that alcohol (or drugs) is almost certainly becoming a real problem.

1. Do you think about drinking even when you are straight?
2. Do you miss days/class periods at school because of drinking?
3. Do you drink to overcome shyness and build confidence?
4. Is drinking affecting your reputation?
5. Do you drink to escape from study or home worries?
6. Have you gotten into trouble at home because of drinking?
7. Does it bother you if someone says you drink too much?
8. Do you feel guilty after drinking?
9. Do you do without other things so you can buy liquor?
10. Is drinking more important than eating?
11. Have you lost any friends since you began drinking?
12. Do your old friends drink less than you do?
13. Are you going with a crowd of heavy drinkers?
14. Do you drink until the bottle or the beer cans are all dead?
15. Have you ever had a loss of memory from drinking, including waking up in the morning and wondering what happened the night before?
16. Do you make up stories to cover up your drinking?

17. Have you ever been stopped for drunken driving?
18. Do you get annoyed with classes or lectures on drinking?
19. Do you drink alone?
20. Do *you* think you have a problem with drinking?

The "warning signs" for a drinking or drug problem are similar to symptoms of depression — sudden personality changes or wide mood swings — a happy communicative girl who is now sullen and angry, or a placid, quiet teenager who all of a sudden is giggly and incoherent. Is she more sensitive to criticism than she has been, more distrustful, hostile? Will she now do anything, *be* anyone to impress her peers?

You may realize that she never brings her friends home, that you no longer even know who her friends are. Or perhaps there are new problems of adjustment in school, where before there were none to speak of.

How can you help her? First of all, don't deny the problem or arrange your life to accommodate it. Neither will it help if you feel responsible for or guilty about your daughter's problem, nor blame her for everything that's wrong with the family. It won't help to try to force her to change her behavior through threats or manipulation, preaching or nagging. None of those things will encourage her to give up the only thing that may be making her feel good now.

She needs your love, understanding, and support, and the first step is to bring the problem out in the open. You need not know what to do or say; you *do* need to communicate your caring, and an attitude of "Let's see how we can work this out together."

Don't be afraid to let your daughter know you aren't

comfortable having her stoned or drunk in your house. (Never try to reason with her when she is "out of it.") As one loving mother told her daughter, "I can't force you to do what pleases me, but if there is to be any peace here, we have to work something out. It disrupts everyone else's life when you are so out of it."

If you find pot or a liquor bottle in your daughter's room, she is trying to tell you something, says John Bolf. She may be trying to get attention or shock you. It's important not to make the mistake of focusing on the incident itself, but instead to look at where the pain is really coming from, whether it is from within or outside of the family.

The Baxter family had to face their daughter's alcohol abuse and their own reluctance to admit there could be any real problems in their household.

"When we could no longer ignore that Debbie was an alcoholic — and, believe me, you can find all kinds of ways to ignore the obvious when you are scared to death of it — we talked to our minister, who told us about a program in our area. We all went to a therapist together," said Mary Baxter, Debbie's mother.

"Debbie isn't drinking anymore, but we know that life still isn't easy for her. We didn't always realize that; we just always used to thank God that we had such a good little girl who gave us no trouble. We didn't notice her hurting, and she was afraid to let us know that she didn't always *feel* like a good girl.

"We thought we had open communication, but I guess a lot went unsaid in our home. We talk more now, and things aren't as quiet as they were before Debbie brought the pain — which we learned is there to some extent in every family — to our attention. Now we know that quiet doesn't always mean peaceful.

"We'll all make it through her adolescence — though Lord knows it's harder because the dope and the booze are *there*, everywhere Debbie turns."

Just as parents can help their children resist the peer pressure to be sexual before they are ready to handle the consequences, so too can we help them withstand the pressure to become involved with drugs and alcohol. Young people may need to be reminded of the simple fact that they have the right *not* to drink or smoke, no matter who else is. And they don't have to apologize to anyone for not drinking. A simple "no thanks," without a lot of explanation, will suffice; anything more might seem as if they are embarrassed or unsure of their decision.

You might suggest your daughter consider these questions: "Am I trying to impress certain friends with my drinking/drug-taking? If so, who? And, are those friends worth it?"

"Many teenagers who drink heavily are at a disadvantage because, unlike hard-core adult alcoholics or addicts, they haven't yet hit bottom," says John Bolf. "They probably still have their health. They think they can stop drinking any time they want to. They have little concept of the future, nor do they realize that booze or drugs are destroying that future."

To help insure the future, it may well be necessary to seek outside help. An important point to remember is that the most successful therapy treats both the alcohol or drug problem itself while also looking at the errors in thought and the values that resulted in the abuse. And, again, since the substance abuse is often a symptom of some pain in the family, family therapy may be in order.

If your daughter has a problem with drugs and alcohol, or if you just want more information, the following organizations and agencies can be very helpful:

• National Clearinghouse for Alcohol Information, Box 2345, Dept. 10, Rockville, MD 20852. An arm of the National Institute on Alcohol Abuse and Alcoholism, the Clearinghouse has information on all aspects of alcohol use and abuse. It also has listings of state and community information, counseling and treatment facilities.

• Alcoholics Anonymous, P.O. Box 459, Grand Central Station, New York, NY 10017. Al-Anon Family Groups, 115 East 23rd Street, New York, NY 10017. Information and referral to community services; local chapters are listed in telephone directories. And as Dr. John Bolf says: "A.A. may be an important part of the treatment of a teenage alcoholic. It's good for her to hear the stories of other alcoholics. She can identify with those her own age, and find out that drinking can only lead to endless despair and ruined lives at any age." Parents of teens with drinking problems might well contact Al-Anon, the national organization for family members of alcoholics, whose aim is to help understand, live with and assist the drinker overcome her problem.

• National Council on Alcoholism, Inc., 733 Third Avenue, New York, NY 10017. The NCA has a list of organizations in many cities that can refer you to doctors and clinics that provide treatment for alcoholism. Some local NCA chapters offer counseling and treatment.

• Family Service Association of America, 14 East 23rd Street, New York, NY 10010. Advises on therapy that treats problem drinking as a concern of the whole family.

• Parent-Teachers Association. Contact your local chapter to see if they are taking part in the PTA's Alcohol Education Project. NIAAA-funded, the program focuses on preventive education and awareness and peer counseling. The aim is to help parents, teachers, and young people look at their own attitudes regarding alcohol and to assist teens in making realistic, informed decisions about drinking.

Many high schools and local free clinics offer drug and alcohol programs which use peer counselors. Their emphasis is often on resolving problems of loneliness and alienation, which may manifest in substance abuse.

# 10

## *Anorexia: Diet without End*

THE EMACIATED LITTLE GIRL HUDDLED in a small corner of the giant hospital bed. She had eaten nothing for over a week. Although most of the time she was semicomatose from the effects of near-malnutrition and dehydration, she was anchored down by heavy canvaslike straps across her chest and knees. Her right arm was even more tightly secured because she was being fed intravenously and would, if she were able, rip the needle from her arm.

It had taken the twelve-year-old-who-looked-nine just two months to lose thirty pounds. Her almost transparent skin was stretched over her tiny angular skeleton. Most of her face was hidden beneath a tangled mass of reddish hair. But her eyes could be discerned, betraying the fact that she was very much alive. They were rats' eyes, sharp with the dull brilliance peculiar to desperate hunger. But she was no longer aware of her need for food, nor was she aware that she was starving herself to death. She was even unaware that she was silently screaming for someone to help her find a way out of the darkness that was eating her up alive.

Twenty-one years ago, I was that bewildered, bewildering child. Though it was documented as far back as Biblical times, it seems I "contracted" a disease before its time, at least before the time when it became important enough to find its way onto TV talk shows. When I had anorexia nervosa in the winter of 1960 — the winter I was unwillingly thrust into puberty — few had heard of it. I was sufficiently unique that my case was written up in journals and presented at medical conventions, and that the doctors and other medical and psychological personnel whom I encountered didn't quite know what to do with me.

But, as I have said (and said) before, times have changed for women, and as they have, it has been no coincidence that in less than ten years, the incidence of anorexia has skyrocketed by an amazing 1,000 percent, until, according to those who keep such records, one in 300 adolescent females in this country is the victim of the diet without end.

For anorexia is almost entirely an adolescent female–specific malady: 95 percent of all anorexics are females, usually from middle- to upper-middle-class families, between the ages of thirteen and nineteen — either on their way into, solidly entrenched in, or on their uncertain way out of adolescence. Up to 20 percent of these young women will die.

Defined simply, anorexia nervosa is a loss of appetite caused by emotional conflict or disturbance. But, in reality, there is nothing very simple about this illness, this total dedication to self-starvation. Its symptoms and consequences are certainly far from easy. Today, anorexia often begins as a diet to lose five or ten pounds (few of the girls start out noticeably overweight), but at some point the psychological brakes to dieting falter and give out.

At first, the anorexic girl may appear to be the typical teenager, flitting from one fad diet to another. But she will continue to cut out foods systematically, ending up eating only seven lettuce leaves or two egg whites a day. She often goes on eating binges, and then to purge herself of the food and the guilt, will force herself to vomit or take excessive amounts of laxatives and diuretics. The object becomes to consume virtually no calories. To this end, she may become extremely active — doing pushups, running, getting very little sleep — pushing herself until anyone else would drop. And then she goes some more.

The anorexic has a tremendous fear that once she starts eating, she will be unable to stop. She thinks about, dreams about food constantly, actually making it inaccurate to associate anorexia with loss of appetite. It would be far more correct to say that the hunger is ignored, crushed, thrown out. She may be very hungry indeed, but simply be completely out of touch with whatever messages her body is trying to communicate to her. She may even cook huge gourmet meals for her family, taking a sort of vicarious satisfaction from watching them eat.

She has an extremely distorted body image. No matter how much she looks like an inmate of a concentration camp — a common description of anorexics — she will look in the mirror and see that she is fat, and needs to lose more.

If she loses enough weight — 20 percent to a third or more of her total body weight is common — she will become amenorrheic (her periods will cease), the hair on her head will begin to fall out, though she may gain a soft downy fuzz on other parts of her body. She may become jaundiced in appearance, and her legs may swell. There will be a slowing down of her circulatory system, and her other bodily functions may start to shut down. The muscles can waste away, as the body, in a desperate search for protein, begins to feed upon itself, damaging her kidneys and other organs.

Just as the physical consequences of this illness are many and far-reaching, so are the meanings behind it. And even though far more girls are deep into drugs and booze, are becoming mothers before their time, and are taking what appear to be far more drastic steps to put an end to their lives, it may be that no other phenomenon can tell us as much about the painful side of growing up female right now than can anorexia.

But that might not be easily apparent if you are getting all of your information about anorexia from newspapers and talk shows. As usual, they are opting for the answers that grab the most readers or viewers, and can be swallowed and digested without the need to look very deeply into ourselves. Thus, we are being handed the rather pat notion that the chief cause of anorexia, in its current appalling proportions, is our idealization of the female form as pencil-thin. To hear them tell it, designer jeans are almost singlehandedly responsible for the dieting disease. (I can almost see the headlines: "Gloria Vanderbilt and Calvin Klein Responsible for Death of Thousands of Teenage Girls.")

While it is true that our love affair with skinny pants that have the names of the famous and the would-be famous stitched on the rear has led many of us to swear off cheesecake and potato chips, it is far too simplistic to say that thousands of young women would diet to death over them, and let the matter go at that. For, according to Dr. Hilde Bruch, professor of psychiatry at Baylor College of Medicine in Houston, a respected authority on anorexia:

"Starvation is merely a symptom and not the real problem. It's just a smoke screen. The real illness has to do with the way these girls feel about themselves."

And the way these girls feel about themselves is, at least in part, the result of the painfully rigid standards of perfection — much more far-reaching than merely the physical realm — which society has established for them in the last few liberated years.

Here again we tend to send our daughters terribly mixed-up messages. "Go out in a man's world and be strong and self-reliant, but do it in a size 5 body. Go for it, but watch out that the package you are going in is not too muscular, not too sturdy, else someone might be threatened."

So while the anorexic girl may be trying the only way she can to attain this dualistic ideal of the new feminine faultlessness, she may, at the same time, be running from it, this time not through drugs or having babies, but by denying herself the basic stuff of life that allows her bones and muscles to become strong and adult. To put it another way, when the world seems to offer vast new opportunities to a young woman, without making it safe for her to test them out, it may seem like a much better idea to remain a little girl.

In her book *The Golden Cage,* Dr. Bruch writes what by now for us has become a familiar, though no less disturbing, refrain: "Growing girls can experience liberation as a demand and feel that they *have* to do something outstanding. Many of my patients have expressed the feeling that they are overwhelmed by the vast number of potential opportunities available to them which they 'ought' to fulfill, that there were too many choices and they had been afraid of not choosing correctly. One compared the demands pressing in on a modern teenage girl to the pressures a forty-year-old executive might experience before he breaks down with a heart attack."

So, when the world demands more than she thinks she is up to, one thing a young girl can prove she can excel at is to become the thinnest of them all. At least in this one way, no one can say she is ordinary or average.

One very skinny thirteen-year old, who is still waging a fight to add life-sustaining meat to her frail bones, told me how it started for her. "I kept thinking, 'I don't contribute enough. People don't recognize me enough. I don't get enough respect or attention or praise.' Looking back, I can see that there was another thought — one that I really wasn't anywhere near *aware* I was thinking — it was 'People will notice me if I lose a lot of weight.'

"Every time I stepped on the scales and saw that I had lost another pound, I was so proud. I felt like I had accomplished something important. I was different and I was winning. Gaining an ounce was admitting defeat."

Then again, if a girl feels she cannot measure up to some amorphous new standard of perfection as the status quo, perhaps if she becomes insignificant in size (as she already is in self-concept), no one will ask anything of her, for she will have virtually disappeared.

In addition, anorexia is also frequently an attempt to deny sexuality in a time and place that insists that young girls wear and use theirs early, often long before they are ready. Hilde Bruch points out that the anorexia can appear "after a film or lecture on sex education which emphasizes what she should be doing, but is not ready to do."

So she makes herself sexually unattractive and unapproachable. As already stated, her menses cease and her form loses whatever female roundness it had acquired, thus seeming to turn the clock back to an easier and more innocent girlhood.

"I developed early and I hated it when boys began to whistle and say things to me about my body," said one "recovering" anorexic. "I didn't know what I was supposed to do. I decided to go on a diet so I could look more like the other thirteen-year-olds. I did not want to look sexy. The more I began to look like the old, the little, Ingrid, the more I liked it."

Anorexia can also be a girl's expression of the desire to be in control in a world where she feels as if she has control over very little. At least she alone can very carefully monitor what she chooses to put into her body.

"In a sense," says Vivian Kaplan, "anorexics are trying to control nature. They are trying to control their own body's message to refuel and its attempt to grow. They are trying to control the way others see them and treat them. And, in the extreme, the young person may be trying to control, or dare, mortality itself: 'Look how far I can go without dying.'" For very few of these girls actually want to die.

As with a pregnancy or a suicide attempt, anorexia can be a cry for attention, a way of telling a family who has trouble listening to more direct messages that she needs help. And the anorexic girl often does come from an environment in which communication has been faltering or one in which another family member — usually, but not always, a sibling — has traditionally garnered most of the attention.

But, then, she never seemed to require a lot of notice. She had always done what was asked of her, and often more. She may have been a bit on the shy, docile side, but she was probably bright, verbal, funny. She always seemed to be quite able to take care of herself, and also of the adults around her. Her grades had always been a source of parental pride.

She had always been a sweet, obedient girl — a thoroughly good girl. But in her own eyes, she has not been good enough, and she is afraid that someone will discover what a fraud she has been, how really nasty and mean she can be.

But then she begins to think, if only I could lose *enough* weight. . . . Somehow goodness becomes synonymous with pounds lost.

In contrast to the homes of other troubled girls, hers has had a paucity of crises — at least the kind that show up in columns of statistics. Hilde Bruch says that only a very few of the patients with whom she has worked over the years have come from homes where parents were divorced or even spoke about marital difficulties. There are no records of physical or mental or alcohol or any other sort of abuse. Usually, there has been no lack of the material goods we have come to believe make us happy.

These homes have traditionally been upper-middle-class, though, as researchers are noting, the level of social and financial position of the "average" family of an anorexic is broadening to include some from the lower middle class, at least those that, as Bruch points out, are very "upwardly mobile and achievement-oriented." It is apparent that, as the push for perfection and the determination not to miss out on anything now available to women (including, but not limited to, owning a figure straight out of *Vogue*) is becoming more attractive and accessible to the less "advantaged," families farther down the socioeconomic line are becoming more susceptible to the maladies of those who are accustomed to the "good" things.

"These families have moved up a notch or two in the world from where their parents were," says psychologist Marilyn Mehr. "And there is an expectation that their daughters will do the same.

"But often the parents themselves feel like impostors, as if they don't really belong up there. They have to keep up a front, keep looking good so that they won't be found out. And the feeling of family may get lost in the constant pretense of always looking outside to see how they are measuring up. The daughter picks up on this charade, and learns very quickly that it is a good idea not to let her parents know that she is not as good as she is also busy pretending.

"Frequently, everyone in the family is attempting to maintain some sort of pretense. It may not be considered good manners to express anger or other 'negative' emotions. No matter what their status, parents often do not feel good about themselves or what they have accomplished in life, and their daughters often believe it is up to them to make up for all that." (As Bruch notes, more than two-thirds of these families have only female children. When there are sons, they are often far apart in age from the anorexic daughter.)

The mother or the father or both often feel they have had to sacrifice their own dreams to raise their families. As Vivian Kaplan says: "These parents are good people, hard workers, the salt of the earth. But they feel as if they have missed out on something. And, for various reasons, they put too much value — often including great emphasis on what she does or does not eat — on the child who turns out to be anorexic. And, even though they probably never said so explicitly, this child has grown up believing she is obligated to pay them back, to live up to their ideal of her."

And she really does not feel capable of doing that. We have already seen how damaging it is when a young girl feels she is not good enough to live up to expectations — the ones others have for her and those she has internalized, perhaps magnified, and made her own.

There is strain in these families — seldom open fighting, but a buzzing undercurrent of disharmony. Members rarely say what they really think or feel, instead offering their interpretations of what they are sure everyone else is trying to say. No one ever really knows what is going on or where he stands with anyone else. That is an emotionally precarious way to live.

"It is difficult in such an atmosphere to know what is real," says Marty Wasserman, a psychologist who works with anorexics and their families. "These girls grow up trying to second-guess what others want of them, not even asking what they want for themselves. They are living up to an image underneath which they have no conviction of their own worthiness."

That there are few divorces, but many unhappy marriages, is not surprising. These people are too dependent on each other to leave. By the time a girl stops eating, she is very frequently calling attention not only to her own pain but to the whole dysfunctional family system. Being as good as she can be has not made her parents happy or their marriage a good one. Maybe — just maybe — she can do something else (and this is *not* a conscious calculation) that will work better.

The anorexic girl can not go to her parents and say, "I'm hurting," or "I see some problems here that bear working on." She probably not only feels she should not be laying her pain on her already overburdened parents, she is not willing to blow her whole pretense at being the perfect kid. If that is all she has, she cannot afford to lose that pseudo-self-image.

Vivian Kaplan, who became my therapist when I was twelve years old and couldn't bring myself to eat, recently explained something to me that I think is apropos for so many other anorexic girls today: "Under the guise of illness, you could say what you felt was unacceptable to say verbally: 'Mom and Dad, I'm not happy. I'm tired of trying to be good, of being thought of as wiser than most adults. I'm only a kid.' Doing it the way you did, no one could think you were responsible, and you could engender everyone's pity and affection, while avoiding their anger and rejection.

"Your illness was also an indirect expression of your own anger, as illnesses often can be. And it was a signal for help. You had to do it in a rather dramatic way, or you would not have been heard. You said to yourself — not consciously — 'I can't stand the way things are going, and it won't work if I go to my parents and say, "I am unhappy," ' because *they* were not particularly happy. That probably would not have been reason enough to bring you to therapy or make any significant changes in the way you were living."

That is a tremendously valuable observation — not only for me, but for so many other young women. It is difficult for parents to accept that there could be anything seriously wrong with their daughter, and it is difficult, as I've said, for the young woman herself to bring her hurt out into the open. Very often, when young people go to their parents and say, "I'm worried," a loving parent will say, "Honey, there's really nothing to worry about." Even if a child could say, "I'm really afraid that my life will always be this unhappy," how many well-intentioned parents might reply, "Time heals all." Or if a child could muster up the courage (or the awareness) to say, "I feel really ugly, outside and inside," mightn't a parent who herself has gone through the awkwardness of adolescence tell her daughter, "You are a late bloomer," or "You are beautiful to me."

Sometimes much more is needed than those sorts of reassurances. But for many families, those are the only tools they have learned to work with.

Oftentimes, when an anorexic girl is finally brought in for treatment — and it is common for her to have lost a tremendous amount of weight before anyone can admit there is a problem — both the patient and her family will tell helping personnel that, apart from this little eating problem, things at home are just fine.

In fact, while parents often secretly blame themselves for their daughter's anorexia, openly they are often unwilling to accept any responsibility for it, and may resent anyone who points out to them the other flaws in the family system. An open power struggle often develops for the first time between parents and daughter, the apparent object of which is to get her to eat. Underneath that may be the young girl's attempt, also for the first time, to direct her own life, to begin to separate her own needs and dreams and choices from those of her parents. And the way she begins to lay claim to those things may be to start with a simpler premise: "This is *my* body."

My own mother can look back over twenty years and, with some small amount of detachment, remember what my illness was like for her: "When you stopped eating, we reasoned with you. We begged. Finally, we threatened. Nothing worked, and I didn't know what to do. I was, all at once, so scared, angry, and frustrated. I was aware of how much I loved you, and was afraid I was going to lose you and that, in a way I couldn't understand, it would be my fault. But, in another way, I also think I hated you for what you were doing to the rest of us."

My mother's anger would seem to be a normal response, but anyone who has never accepted her own anger may feel especially ashamed at being angry with this pitifully skinny "little" girl. Parents, nonetheless, *are* angry. As Virginia Satir tells me, this anger comes from the cold realization that they can't make their formerly loving, docile daughter do a simple thing like eat. Also, this now obstinate, even hostile, creature is not allowing them to maintain their self-image as good parents. (Remember, that is often the most positive view these individuals have of themselves.)

When I had anorexia, I was a trailblazer of sorts, and, thus, no one knew quite what to do with me. There were no newspaper articles my parents could refer to and say, "Oh, so *that's* what she's got, and *this* is how she can be helped." The old family doctor, who was from a very old school indeed, recommended I be given regular spankings and be made to do dishes and clean toilets until I came to my senses.

My parents sensibly switched to another doctor, who, after giving me a battery of medical tests to determine whether there was an organic basis to my complaints of stomach pains, suggested I be taken to a child psychiatrist. (My anorexia did not start with a diet, but with a tonsil-lectomy, after which I said my throat, and then my stomach, hurt too much to eat.)

While it was very difficult for my parents to admit that I needed that kind of help, they loved me and of course they took me. I was frightened that I really was crazy, and when the psychiatrist said that if I was not hospitalized I might die, I was petrified. I had seen *Snake Pit*, with Olivia de Havilland, and I was sure that was where I would wind up.

Instead, I was admitted to Children's Hospital, in Los Angeles, on a general medical floor. At that time, not only were there no special treatment programs for anorexics at Children's; there was no adolescent unit at all. At various times, I shared my room with an eighteen-month-old boy with pneumonia and a seven-year-old girl with leukemia. In contrast to these "truly" sick kids, many of the medical staff did look on me as "crazy" or as a mean, spiteful girl who was choosing to make herself sick and everyone else frustrated.

Not knowing how else to handle me, medical personnel tried to get me to eat by coaxing, bribing, rationalizing, and threatening. Reading their nametags, I quickly became familiar with each of them and their functions. When one of them told me what I was supposed to do, I would say, "Yes, but Dr. So-and-so told me it would be all right if I did this."

"You had everyone running in circles," laughed Vivian Kaplan, "but for all anorexics, getting people to do what they want becomes a test of their strength and of their lovableness."

At that moment in my life, Vivian Lichter Kaplan, the young determined redhaired psychologist, was my saving. At first, she was assigned only to give me a block of psychological tests. ("Do these tests prove I am psychotic?" I asked suspiciously. "No." I remember her smiling at my use of the word. "I doubt whether you are even 'neurotic.' Your thinking is too clear about exactly what it is that will get you the help you need.")

Since she was the only one I seemed to respond to at all,

she became my therapist. "I had never worked with anyone with anorexia before," says Kaplan. "So I went back and read as much literature as I could find. I only know I loved the fight in you, the struggle to say, 'I want to be.' We related to each other, and I guess I was too stupid to be scared.

"I came on strong with you from the beginning, because I sensed that you were a frightened kid who needed to know what the parameters were. You needed someone to say, 'Hey, cut it out. You don't need to hurt yourself any-more.'"

Much of my early therapy consisted of learning to give myself permission to have anger and to express it. It petri-fied me when I could no longer hide from myself the fact that much of the blackness that filled me up — leaving no room for taking in healthy forms of nourishment — was anger. I had never really been angry at my parents, at least not outwardly. Very good little girls simply do not do that, especially not with parents who always, always loved them and gave them everything they could.

As Vivian Kaplan explained to me: "You knew your parents were trying very hard. It must have made you phenomenally guilty to have any anger toward them. It was much easier for you to turn that anger inward, on yourself."

Unfortunately, I had anorexia before the time when it became common for the patient to be seen with her family in therapy. The only "therapy" my parents received was a few brief sessions with a well-meaning psychiatric social worker, in which the emphasis was definitely on "how to handle Janet when she gets home." My parents came away from those sessions angry, frustrated, and more guilty than ever before.

Today, family therapy is considered one of the most important tools in the treatment of anorexia nervosa. As Hilde Bruch writes: "The development of anorexia nervosa is so closely related to patterns of family interaction that successful treatment must always involve resolution of the underlying family problems. . . . There is no rule on how to handle this, except for one generalization: clarification of the underlying family problem is a necessary part of treatment. Parents tend to present their family life as more harmonious than it actually is, or they deny difficulties altogether. All anorexics are involved with their families in such a way that they have failed to achieve a sense of independence."

So, the anorexic is speaking, through her symptoms, for the rest of the family. Often, food and the patient's weight are taboo subjects in family therapy, so that the scrapegoat symptom will no longer be center stage. Such therapy also stresses that what the girl eats is her business alone. And, since for many of these families, everyone's business has become everyone else's, emphasis is placed on teaching all members to allow each other privacy and autonomy in other matters.

The objective of family therapy is to bring to light long-held secrets or ambivalent communications, do away with the sometimes phony "niceness" that has killed real joy, make it all right for members to function independently of each other, and allow the family system to loosen up and members to accept each other for who they truly are and want to be.

"Since families often resist the view that says the system itself, not the 'identified patient,' is the problem, they may want to end therapy as soon as possible," says Marilyn Mehr. "When the kid has gotten to a safer weight and is getting ready to be discharged from the hospital, they often have the attitude, 'We'll do better when we get her home.' Since the severity of the problem has been diminished, they don't want to continue in outpatient family therapy. But that is an erroneous assumption — the symptoms have merely been controlled.

"We also see a lot of resistance several weeks into the family therapy, when some of the deeper underlying issues have come up and it begins to become very painful."

Usually, along with the family therapy, the young woman is also seen in individual therapy, which aims to help her realize that she will not lose control over her life if she regains a normal weight; that it is acceptable to have weaknesses and "negative" emotions; that she is not required to live her life for anyone else; that she is a unique individual, worthy of loving, no matter what she weighs or what she accomplishes.

Behavior modification is another therapy that is frequently used in the treatment of anorexia patients. This often entails the making of a contract between medical and psychiatric personnel on the one side and the patient on the other. For instance, if she gains a specified amount of weight she will earn specific rewards, like being able to use the phone, watch television, or have visitors. If she loses weight, she is faced with loss of such privileges or the prospect of being tube-fed through the nose.

Hospitalization is, of course, necessary to ensure that the patient is holding up her end of the contract. Along the way, it is hoped that the patient will learn new eating habits.

In the short run, this method does seem to work: many patients do gain weight. But there are a number of psychiatrists and psychologists who are dead set against behavior modification, saying that, at best, its benefits are temporary and that it reinforces the notion that anorexia is an illness of appetite and weight, which in reality it is not.

Vivian Kaplan points out that behavior modification, in the long run, may actually cause more psychological problems. "Behavioral conditioning does appear to work well," she agrees, "but afterward these kids are often left more confused and angry than ever before. We have 'fooled' them into giving up the last bit of control they had over their own lives, and we have progressed no farther into real insight."

How does a parent detect a potentially anorexic daughter? The problem is obvious if dieting becomes an obsession; if her taste in foods seems irrational; if she takes laxatives, diuretics, or vomits after meals (although she may keep those things secret).

But the problem does not have to reach that point for parents to become aware there is a problem. As all of the professionals I talked to agreed, there is the potential for serious trouble when a child never, never causes any trouble. I do not mean to imply that getting all A's or being a kind, giving person is a cause for alarm. It is a matter of degree that is the problem.

"It is the extra push," says Hilde Bruch, "the being not good, but 'better,' that makes the significant difference between these unhappy youngsters who starve themselves and other adolescents who are capable of enjoying life. True prevention requires that their pleasing superperfection is recognized early as a sign of inner misery."

If you have any further questions about anorexia, you may want to write the National Anorexia Society, Box 29461, Columbus, Ohio, 43229.

And it might tell us something to listen to Kelly, a seventeen-year-old, bright but, by the new standards, not brilliant, girl. At 5′5″, she has gone from 125 to 80 pounds in an attempt to create a new "image" for herself. After hospitalization and intensive therapy, she is a pleasing but somewhat bony 107. She has also gained a sense of perspective and appreciation for who she is.

"I was scared to death of being ordinary, average — in other words, nobody. I wanted to do things my parents were never able to do, only I didn't really know how. When I was eating less than anybody else, I did get this feeling of superiority. But it wasn't enough. Not nearly enough. Because I still didn't like *me*.

"It's strange, here you are feeling 'one up' on all those pigs who can't help stuffing their faces. But deep down, you don't feel really good about who you are. So, you keep on not eating, because by now, that's all that is left.

"I've learned a lot about myself since I've been in therapy. I've learned to like myself without having to do something spectacular to prove I'm worth it. Don't let anyone kid you. It is a horrible burden to think you need to be special, better than anyone else. Because in the process, you lose yourself."

In the next chapter, we will look at how other teenage girls are taking even more drastic measures to lose themselves, and how we can help them.

# 11

## A Cry for Help

Ann Arbor, Michigan (June 14, 1979) (UPI) Agnes Vass, a 17-year old senior who learned she would not graduate with her Huron High School classmates, put a .22-caliber rifle to her heart and killed herself, police said.

The girl was found dead Tuesday on the school's athletic field, where she had starred in field hockey. Her hockey stick and the rifle lay beside her body.

Howard Harris, Ann Arbor school superintendent, said Agnes tried to tell her parents during the weekend that she was going to fail the required English course. "She couldn't," he said.

"The parents were most understanding, most understanding," Harris said, after a counselor, at the request of the girl, called Steven and Agnes Vass and told them young Agnes had failed.

Her body was discovered by a jogger early Tuesday. Police said she left a handwritten suicide note at home, saying how upset she was over her grades.

Police went to the Vass home in suburban Pittsfield Twp. after the girl's body was found. "What a waste, what a waste," Steven Vass told police.

One young life lost is a terrible waste. Multiply that loss by several thousand and the expense is incalculable. Mental health professionals are now calling the phenomenon of teenage suicide a national epidemic.

Each year, some 5,000 teens and young adults in this country — many from what we like to think of as "average," and even "above average" families — take their own lives. That is three times as many as a single generation ago — an increase that far outstrips suicides in any other age group. (Only "accidents" claim more young lives.)

And, as mentioned in the Introduction, girls are not only closing the gap in the number of completed suicides — they now comprise 40 percent of the total — but they are also beginning to ape boys in the "macho" methods of self-destruction they are employing. As psychiatrist Victor Victoroff has said, there is a frightening new level of despondency among girls, one that is prompting some of them to turn down "avenues of no return."

What's more, the actual suicides represent only the tip of a huge iceberg of emotional distress, because an estimated 400,000 young people make "unsuccessful" attempts to die every year.

Girls make almost three-quarters of those attempts. Why have there been so many "failed" female attempts at self-destruction? The trend toward androgynous sex-role behavior notwithstanding, experts agree that it is still more acceptable for females to show emotion and to exhibit a need for help. So a young girl's half-hearted suicide attempt often is a way of pleading, "I don't really want to do this, but I *must* make you know how desperate I am."

Still, even all of these shocking facts and figures may be far too conservative. Some of the experts are saying that there are two to three suicides for every one recorded, because a great number of fatal and near-fatal accidents are actually "subintentioned" suicides in which an angry or depressed teenager takes unnecessary life-threatening risks, like driving recklessly or mixing drugs and alcohol. And there is no doubt that "risk-taking" behavior has most definitely become a new prerogative of the once gentler sex.

In addition, it is not at all rare for a family doctor to obscure the cause of a young person's death to spare the family the shameful stigma attached to suicide.

Which kids are killing themselves? More Protestants than Jews, more Jews than Catholics. In the North, a larger proportion of blacks; in the South, more whites. In general, more city teenagers commit suicide. April is indeed the cruelest month when it comes to suicide; the period immediately before Christmas comes a close second. More young people take their lives on blue Monday (the pressure of returning to school?) and on Friday (dateless date night?) than on any other days.

We have already talked about some of the factors that are creating so much pain for our daughters, how the still-formless opportunities for young women have also brought new pressures. How they hear that success means *male* success and how that success, clearly, has not brought real joy to that sex.

It is true that I have said these things, in one form or another, before. But, because we are talking about so many young women taking or attempting to take their lives, they bear repeating.

To capsulize what I have said earlier: our daughters are being asked to find out who they are and what they are about within a culture that is itself having a severe identity crisis. The family as a microcosmic unit of society is now fragile and uncertain. There is a pervading ethic that to feel good, and feel good right *now*, is the first inalienable right. Because, after all, tomorrow will probably bring more pollution and shortages, both material and spiritual.

And, if all that were not quite enough to drive the young to despair, there is that double message we are sending them: you teenagers are a bunch of troubled statistics and we aren't particularly crazy about you. On the other hand, because we are so uncertain of what is really important about life, and because we are afraid of getting old and dying, we will emulate you and hope that youth is catching.

Still, suicide is almost always a solution of last resort for a troubled teen, chosen only after other alternatives — rebellion, withdrawal, running away, using drugs, delinquency, sometimes even pregnancy — were tried without satisfactory results. Suicide attempters often say that the thought "Maybe this time they'll hear me" accompanied the self-destructive impulse.

Dr. Michael Peck, co-director of the Los Angeles Suicide Prevention Center, agrees: "The vast majority of youngsters who attempt, threaten or commit suicide are not trying to die. They are trying to escape from an unhappy life, and they see death as the only solution to the chronic problem of living."

All of our daughters have grown up in these difficult times. But not all of them think of suicide as a logical solution to unhappiness. What separates the girls who can survive and ultimately thrive from those who just can't make it in a society in which the ground rules and the real goodies are so uncertain?

According to most experts, the young people who commit or attempt suicide have experienced more than the average number of "upsets" in their short lifetimes. They have had to put up with more family arguments and unemployment, divorces and remarriages, more illnesses or deaths (including, sometimes, other suicides), more run-ins with the law, more family moves that left close friends behind, and a shaky religious affiliation or identification.

All of these factors contribute to the young person's isolation from meaningful relationships, and it is these important relationships that anchor us to life.

A teenager named Sally provides painful illustration of a child who lost so much she thought there was nothing left to lose. She was only six when her grandmother died. Because both of her parents worked, Nana had always taken care of her. She was the only one the little girl could turn to when she made a new discovery or when she was hurt. After her death, no one else was there to replace that closeness for Sally.

Her parents worked very hard at jobs they didn't like very much, and had little energy left over to devote to her. They saw themselves as life's losers and desperately wanted their daughter to make it for them. And now that women were becoming liberated, they were confident she could fulfill that need about as well as a son might have. Although her aptitude tests showed she was only slightly over average intelligence, Sally's grades were always very high. She sang in her high school glee club and played viola in the orchestra, even though her parents rarely had the time to hear her perform.

By the time Sally reached her teens, her father was drinking heavily. When her parents communicated at all, it was often with short outbursts of anger, and Sally was usually caught in the middle.

In her senior year, Sally's grades slipped enough so that she was not allowed to take part in extracurricular activities. Then Frank, her only real friend, told her he no longer wanted to go steady.

Sally sank deeper and deeper into despondency, but

there was no way she could talk to anyone about how she felt. To do so would mean she was a failure. And she would do anything — anything — not to let the world in on that secret.

So late one night when her parents were asleep, Sally sneaked into the bathroom, found a can of liquid drain cleaner in a cupboard, and somehow downed it all. The next morning, her mother stumbled on Sally's lifeless body on the bathroom floor.

"We gave her everything we could afford," her mother said, defensively. "What more did she want?"

It isn't unusual for loving, well-meaning parents to encourage a child to "make something of herself." But Sally's folks may have pushed too hard — and for unconsciously self-serving reasons. Dr. Richard Seiden, public health professor at the University of California, points out that some parents need their children to achieve to make up for their own feelings of inadequacy.

Some children learn early on that they can win approval only by becoming perfect projections of their parents' fantasies. The parental expectations for suicidal teens often exceed the usual wishes for success that most parents have for their children, and represent a total lack of acceptance of their children as they are.

"The failure of such a child to live up to these expectations," says Michael Peck, "is often experienced as a great humiliation by the child whose superego frequently goes on to make demands of herself even beyond those of the parent — not to mention far beyond her own abilities."

These kids have a sense that *who* they are comes in a poor second — is in fact, extraneous — to what they feel is expected of them.

Along the same lines, some parents try — again, often

unconsciously — to mold their children into a likeness of what they see as their own, idealized selves. When Felice was forty-three, her daughter, Cassandra, turned fifteen. Felice felt her Cassie was much prettier and more self-confident than she had ever been, and so encouraged her to go out with only the best-looking, "most promising" boys in school (the boys *Felice* would have dated had she had the opportunity when *she* was fifteen). It isn't surprising that few boys matched Felice's image of what was good enough for her daughter.

Felice never stopped to think about how Cassandra saw herself. When Cassie was rejected by the shining blond captain of the football team, she attempted suicide. She was found in time, and was put under the care of a psychiatrist, who said Cassie's self-destruction was, in part, a reaction to her mother's intrusiveness. "In a sense, Cassie came to believe that her body — her *self* — belonged more to her mother than it did to her," he said. "Therefore, when she inflicted damage on her body, in a sense, it was really her mother she felt she was hurting."

Such a belief, usually unconscious, is common among suicidal teenagers.

Both Sally and Cassandra fit the "profile" of the suicidal youngster in other ways. Sally had an alcoholic parent, and conflict was a normal state of affairs in her home. Both received inconsistent messages from their parents, messages like "Life was disappointing for me, but you can do better." Such a message leaves a child feeling guilty and unprepared to tackle life for herself.

Both girls were disappointed in love. "It's very common for a love affair gone sour or other major disappointment to precede a suicidal gesture," says Dr. Teicher. "But it is a mistake to believe that that *is* the cause of self-destruction. For most young people, it's only the last straw, the final breakdown of self-esteem." Other circumstances that might serve as "last straws" are a failing grade, a pregnancy, not making a sports team or other activity.

Many parents wonder about the roles of drugs and alcohol in the skyrocketing adolescent suicide rate, and there is disagreement among mental health professionals themselves on this point. Joseph Teicher says there is no real connection between drug use and suicide. Both just happen to be on the rise.

But some experts contend that young suicides actually use drugs less often than do other youngsters. In fact, the absence of drug use may be yet another reflection of the way these kids are cut off from the experiences common to other young people. Still other authorities, however, regard "substance" abuse as a presuicidal clarion cry for help.

Very depressed youngsters have many ways of letting parents know how they feel, and these are warning signs we need to be aware of, says Dr. Calvin Frederick, chief of the National Institute of Mental Health's Disaster and Emergency Mental Health Section. One teenager may have recurrent anxiety attacks. Another may be tired all the time, have no appetite, lose weight, and be unable to sleep (or eat or sleep too much).

A previously good-natured, well-behaved teen may suddenly become disobedient and rebellious — or she may become gloomy, sulky, and unwilling to communicate about anything. She may become extremely bored or restless, or have a series of minor illnesses for which no organic basis can be found.

Depression may also appear as a neglect of schoolwork and a falling off in grades, Withdrawal from friendships, sudden lack of interest in the opposite sex (or, conversely, sudden "promiscuity") may be other signs. Some depressed young people actually ask questions like "What would you do if I weren't here anymore?" or "Do you believe in God (or in life after death)?"

Parents often assume that such "crazy" behavior is just a normal part of the stormy adolescent years. And it may be. But if changes in mood or behavior are sudden, last a long time, or are uncharacteristic of the individual, then notice must be taken.

Suicidal behavior is too often ignored or passed off, especially in young people, as "just a phase." Says one mental health official: "When adolescent depression is unheeded or regarded as merely attention-seeking or a sort of manipulation, young people often escalate their behavior in order to be heard. Frequently, they end up killing themselves when a trained ear or eye should have taken note of the cry for help."

Melanie's cry wasn't heard until it was almost too late. For sixteen of her seventeen years, Melanie had lived up to her mother's ideal of the perfect child. It was during her third year in high school that Melanie seemed to change. She withdrew from school activities, stopped accepting invitations to parties, and didn't seem to care when her grades dropped from A's to C's. She spent much of the time alone in her room, listening to records or just staring at the walls. At meals, she kept silent until her parents, Lois and Jim, gently questioned her about her behavior. Then she got angry and stamped away from the table. When they suggested she see a doctor, she shouted, "Just leave me alone. There is nothing wrong with me."

Then Melanie's black moods seemed to depart as suddenly as they'd arrived. In recent months, she had been quiet, but never surly, her grades were up, and her parents were immensely relieved to have the "good" Melanie back.

One morning, not long before Melanie's graduation from high school, Lois poked her head into her daughter's room to awaken her. When Melanie didn't answer, Lois' eyes traveled to the nightstand, where she saw a bottle of her tranquilizers. What was her prescription doing in Melanie's room? Then she spotted the note next to the bottle.

A sudden wave of nausea hit Lois. She picked up the piece of pale blue stationery: "Dear Mom and Dad . . . I'm sorry . . . didn't mean to cause . . . just too hard . . . not your fault . . . I'm not good enough. . . ." Frantically, Lois examined the bottle. The last time she'd seen it, it had been well over half full. Now it was empty. She screamed.

Melanie survived. Today she is finding help from a psychologist she likes and from a family shocked into awareness of their daughter's inner turmoil. But only a few desperate minutes kept Melanie from becoming yet another casualty in the epidemic called teenage suicide.

If you think your child is in pain, don't waste precious time trying to figure out what has gone wrong — or blaming yourself. Neither is this the time to try to convince yourself that your child is not the suicidal "type." While certain backgrounds or behaviors may seem to predispose an adolescent to suicide, statistics aside, no family is immune.

Focus on the many ways you can help. Dr. Frederick and others who work with teens offer some basic guidelines:

• Ask such questions as: "You don't seem to be yourself lately — what's bothering you?" Don't be afraid to ask her if she has ever thought about harming herself. It's unlikely that mentioning suicide to a depressed person will put new ideas into her head. On the contrary, broaching the subject may allow your child to open up and talk about distressing problems. A youngster who hints of suicide may be giving us a chance to keep her alive.

• It is also a myth that the person who attempts and fails at suicide is not serious. Most people who commit suicide have had at least one abortive attempt in their past. Take seriously all suicide threats. Don't believe that people who are talkers are not doers — those who commit the act have often talked about it beforehand. Never dismiss such talk with remarks like "Come on, your problems aren't all that serious" or "You can't possibly mean that."

• Don't try to convince your child that suicide is morally wrong; part of her distress may come from the short supply of morality she sees in the world around her. And it probably would not help to say: "Time heals all wounds." Young people have little evidence that there is any truth in that adage.

• Never try to shock a young person out of suicide. Saying "Go ahead and do it if you feel you have to" becomes a challenge that a distressed and rebellious teen may feel she has to meet.

• Be careful not to intimate that there is something "wrong" with her, or that she is "bad" or "sick" for having despondent or self-destructive feelings, or that she doesn't *need* to feel that way if she would only look on the brighter side of life.

"It doesn't help my daughters if I say, 'You don't have to be lonely or sad or depressed,' because, at that moment, that *is* what they are experiencing," explains Fern Rubin. "I have found it most helpful if I can let them know that I have felt the things they are feeling. Of course, I, too, am lonely and frightened sometimes.

"My job as a mother is not to protect them from their

'negative' ideas or feelings, but to help them clarify them and realize the meaning behind them. And our daughters' suffering is an opportunity for us to look at our own suffering, for the source of their mistaken ideas about the world comes from us in one way or another.''

· Most important, you must really listen to hear the pain behind her words, not merely with your ears, but with all of your understanding. This is not the time to make moral judgments about the ideas or values with which she may be wrestling. Nor is it the time to defend yourself against the anger she may have toward you, nor to feel guilty about her pain. And, no matter what you feel, you must keep your hand outstretched toward her.

Many good, loving parents miss clues, says Calvin Frederick, out of a need to defend themselves. They just don't want to face the unhappy fact that their child might be suicidal. Unconsciously — or consciously — they say to themselves, "I won't let myself think about that.''

If you feel helpless at the idea of talking to your daughter about her depression, you might ask yourself, "What did I need from my mother when I was fifteen or sixteen? And what does my daughter need from me now?" Then talk to her from the position of trying to understand who she is and who you are — not from trying to change her or make her better. Finding what the real issues are is a much more valid concern than finding quick, easy answers.

But all the love you have may not be enough, by itself, to help your child. Don't be afraid to seek outside help. Your family doctor, clergyman, a favorite teacher or school counselor may be able to help or to refer you to someone who can. Most cities and counties have mental health agencies that offer assistance at fees structured to fit a family's income.

If a young person seems to be in immediate danger of harming herself, short-term hospitalization may be the answer. "Often the suicidal teen has lost all sense of attachment to the world," says Dr. Teicher. "The time in the hospital can help reestablish bonds with caring people."

There are over 200 suicide prevention and crisis intervention centers and countless "hot lines" all over the country, staffed twenty-four hours a day by concerned volunteers trained to handle emergencies over the phone. Most of these services refer teens and families to agencies that provide face-to-face treatment.

Listen for a moment to Joan, a sixteen-year old who has scars from razor-blade cuts on her wrists, as well as other, less visible scars. "I didn't really want to die. I just wanted to end the pain and start over. Maybe if parents and kids were kinder to each other, if teachers were more understanding, if we didn't feel so much competition with one another, if our minds weren't so open to sex and closed to true relationships, if we could just love each other for who we are, we would all be better off."

# 12

## *What Does Your Daughter Need from You?*

SINCE THIS WHOLE BOOK has really been about what daughters need from mothers and what mothers can learn from the experience of growing up alongside their daughters in what are, at best, crazy times, this next-to-the-last chapter might well be called "What else your daughter needs from you and can, in the process, teach you."

And she does need a lot from you. Take it from Marjorie, a tall, slim young woman who has been doing quite well as a teenage model for over two years. "What do I need from my mother?" she laughs. "Oh, not much, just complete emotional support and approval and the assurance she'll be there whenever I need her.

"I also need her to help me solve my problems. I need her financial advice. I need to know she'll hold on tight when I want, and let go when I need more freedom. I'm not asking for much, am I?"

Marjorie is not the only girl in town who would like unconditional love and acceptance from her mother. (Don't worry; that does not mean agreeing with everything they say or do, thank goodness.)

Here is an example of what it might mean: Jackie Beaman, who had the difficult task of facing her sixteen-year-old's pregnancy, initially had no idea of how she should handle the problem. Still in shock, all she could think of to say to the frightened girl was: "Tish, I don't like what's happening. I have a lot of feelings I still don't quite understand, but one thing I'm clear on right now is that no matter what you do or where you go, you are always my daughter. I will always love you. That will never change."

That pronouncement didn't make the pregnancy any less real or frightening, but it did open the way for Jackie and Tish to talk. And it may have helped the confused girl see that she didn't have to look beyond her own front door for the kind of love she had been seeking outside.

Later, Jackie told me, "I hated what she had done. I didn't even really like Tish at that moment. But somehow I realized that I didn't always have to admire the things she did or the ways she acted. What is important is that I never stopped loving her essence — her goodness, the spark. And I wanted her to be aware of that."

Such a love — without qualifications, without reservations — says the Reverend Bob Iles, is "so rare and yet so necessary for us to thrive. If young people had a sense of such love, they wouldn't have to go elsewhere to prove that it exists."

We do need — for our sakes and for theirs — to accept our daughters, to love them, even when the masks they are wearing are not particularly lovable. We need to make room for their negative and aggressive feelings and for their mistakes. We need to accept them even during those times when they seem to be rejecting the model we have tried so hard to provide for them. We must try not to take such a rejection personally, and we must remember that it will pass.

"I can't tell you how neat it makes me feel to know that

nothing I could do could make my mother reject me. Nothing," says a seventeen-year-old who considers herself very lucky indeed. "Sometimes both of us are real bitches and we scream and yell at each other. But, bottom line, I know there's no way she doesn't love me, no way she won't be there for me when I need her. And she can count on me the same way."

Along with unconditional love, girls say they covet respect from their mothers and, in turn, they want to be able to respect them.

"It's essential that a mother admire the person her daughter is," says Barbara Hayes, "because the way a young person learns self-respect is through being respected. If a girl comes out of her home feeling good about herself, others pick up on that and treat her accordingly.

"So I would wish that every mother could accept and respect her child as a person, as someone who has been loaned to her, for whom she has responsibility, but who is not her possession."

In fact, establishing a platform of mutual respect is probably even more important than the particular values you seek to pass down to your daughter because, with that solid base, she is more likely to come to you when she has problems with whatever system of values she is struggling with.

What she does not need is for you to try to erase her struggles or to fight her battles for her. Often, we are so eager to give our children happiness, and to protect them from finding what happiness is not, that we may encourage them to avoid what is difficult in life. Instead of asking them to be responsible for their actions, we do *for* them. And, so our daughters frequently don't learn the quality — the gift, really — of being useful and contributing to the world's well-being.

And then we are angry because, all around us, we see a nation of self-indulgent teenagers. But, even worse than that, these are young people who have little confidence that they can cope with life's cranky and constant demands. Is it any wonder that they cut out — sometimes through sex or drugs — sometimes more permanently?

"Don't try to rescue her from everything," says Judith Stevens-Long. "She will never learn anything if you do. She needs to see that what she does has consequences and that she has an effect on the universe, and that the universe has a relationship with her — quite separate from you.

"I would tell my own daughter, 'I have advice I think you might be interested in, but I am not willing to take responsibility for your life.'

"She needs to learn to wrestle life on her own, even if she is thrown. Again. And again. That's hard. That's love."

Young people need to be allowed to make mistakes and they need parents to share the mistakes these adults have made, so that maybe — just maybe — they will have less need to make the same mistakes.

"The most important thing I could ever hope to give my daughter is some perspective to begin to discern what is good for her," says Arlene Epstein. "When she is confused about something, it's tempting to blunder right in there and try to straighten it all out for her. Sometimes I have to try with everything I've got to resist that temptation."

Fern Rubin believes that allowing her daughters the right to be confused may be one of the most loving things she can do for them. "It is really helpful if I can say to them, 'Don't ignore or try to cover up your confusion. Listen to what it is trying to tell you.'

"It takes real effort not to try to take their pain away from them, or to feel that, if you love them enough, you 'should' be able to engender their happiness and security. But if I hold on to that particular 'should,' they may feel they need to be happy for *me* and they will deny their pain.

"But their pain is to be respected as much as their joy, because it points out to them that they have lost something. Once they have seen that, the pain is often no longer necessary."

Another mother states the same case a little differently.

"Katy and I don't always see eye to eye," acknowledges Marcy Graham. "But it's important to me that I respect the choices she makes, even if I wouldn't make the same choices, or even if I don't think they are the right choices. If she doesn't choose my path — which I have to acknowledge may not be the right path for her — I have faith that hers will ultimately be a manifestation of goodness.

"She may have to go through some pain, but there's no way I can take it away from her. And I shouldn't really try."

So, instead of telling your daughter how to handle each conflict, it is probably far more productive to help her to see through the appearance of the problem to the underlying thoughts that are really causing her pain. Don't worry; no mind-reading abilities are required for the job. Such "second sight" is not mystical at all.

For instance, her conflicts, while they may seem to be about sex or grades or birth control or whether the boy next door will call, are often really about loneliness or the need for approval or the fear of failure or that ever-popular existential question, "Am I good enough?" Even though the packaging may appear to be different, are those any different from the issues with which you are dealing?

Indeed, many of the girls I talked to agree that they don't need their mothers to solve their problems for them. But they do want to be able to share their problems and to hear what their mothers have to say.

"I'd like to hear more from my mother about what she really thinks," said one young girl. "Sometimes I feel that she comes on so strong about 'right' and 'wrong' — capital R, capital W — because she's afraid to let me know what she really believes in."

Of course, sharing your beliefs and values does not mean force-feeding her your insights. It is helpful if you can say, "This is the way it looks to me," and then allow her to ponder your "wisdom," modifying it as she needs to, or even throwing it out. In other words, you need to step back, take your "self" out of the way, and let her own ability to respond to intelligence take over.

"For me," admits Fern Rubin, "being as psychological and verbal as I am, the challenge is to say little and trust a lot. Trust what I know to be true — that the individuals who are my daughters are competent, intelligent, beautiful people."

There will be times, of course, when she wants you to tell her what to do, when she wants the easy answer. That's true for all of us. In Maurie Cullen's counseling practice, young people, noticing that her life appears to be rich and full, often figure that what works well for her should, with no script changes, do just as well for them.

Cullen tries hard not to fall into that trap, knowing that any set of hard-and-fast rules, no matter how well-intentioned or time-tested, will not serve these young individuals' growth.

"I try to let them know what is right or wrong for me without indicating they are absolutes," Cullen says. "If a young person asks me something about myself, like, 'Do you smoke marijuana?' or 'Did you have sex before marriage?' I won't lie to her. But first I would like both of us to understand what she really wants by asking that question.

"So I might ask her, 'What would it mean to you if I did (or didn't)?' How would your feelings about me — or yourself — change if I did do that? And does that make it OK for you to do it?'

"I would like young women to realize that it is important to establish their own values, and not to delude themselves that they can adopt mine, at least not without careful consideration. I neither want them to be able to rationalize, 'I can do it because she did,' nor 'She doesn't understand me because she never did it.'

"I would like them to learn that they have a right, as free human beings, to choose a path for themselves, without always relying on the opinions of others, even those whom they love and respect."

Fern Rubin would agree. "I am a guide for my daughter. And a guide is merely someone who walks on the path in front of others. In some ways, that is what I have done. And yet, in other ways, we are walking the same path at the same time. Both of us are working on unresolved dependence, fears, illusions about the way we think it should be. We grow with each other's support, and sometimes seem to grow in spite of each other."

Therefore, what is much more helpful than handing her rights and wrongs on a silver platter is for you simply to be aware of what your values are, what you believe in, what your relationships mean, and what you feel is your responsibility as a human being in this society.

It's important that you should be comfortable with

those values, for you can't help communicating that attitude to your daughter.

"I must confront each issue as it comes up, for myself and for her," says Fern Rubin. "I must let her see that I, too, struggle to see life as clearly as I can, and that she doesn't need to do it for me.

"In a sense, at this point in her life, her consciousness is still an extension of my consciousness. By that, I don't mean that what she does is caused by me, nor can I take credit or blame for who she turns out to be. What I am saying is that if I have certain ideas or values, she will pick up on them. So the clearer I can be about what is moving me to think or act a certain way, the freer she is to do the same.

"Children judge our values by how they see them work, and a teenager who lives in her parents' home will find it difficult to have values that are any clearer than those of her parents."

So daughters need to know you and need you to at least be interested in knowing yourself. One psychologist, in a not unexpected finding, says that adolescent girls whose mothers are interested in self-discovery, who were genuine, empathetic, and liked themselves, were also very likely to score a high self-esteem quotient.

Conversely, Shari Glucoft-Wong has found that when parents don't take care of their own self-esteem issues, or neglect pulling their own lives together, their kids act up around that, either to deflect the pain for their parents, or to rub their noses in it.

One woman whose own mother was always a cloudy enigma to her wants things to be different with her own daughter. "I had no idea of who my mother was," she recalls with sadness. "I had to poke and poke for even the rarest glimpses of what she thought of herself, what was important to her, what she had wanted out of life that she got or failed to get.

"I still feel cheated, and so I really try to let Sammi, my daughter, see me, even when I'm not looking all that good. Perhaps I can help her see who she is by being more who I am, by being a mirror for her, and by letting her know that I have a life apart from her as I know she does from me."

And, as Sammi's mother says, when you let your daughter in on who you are, remember to allow her also to see you when you aren't "looking all that good." Contrary to the old rules, in which a parent was not supposed to share her doubts with her child because the child would lose respect for the parent's authority or adultness, now we know that such genuine sharing benefits us all. In fact, one of the greatest gifts a mother can bestow on her daughter is the simple acknowledgment that she isn't Superperson, and that, therefore, her child is not obligated to leap tall buildings at a single bound.

It is a tremendous relief to know that Mother doesn't always have to know best, and that there are real questions that are not easy for anyone to answer, choices that may never be completely clear-cut.

As one wise young lady found out: "I finally realized my mom doesn't know it all. She doesn't have to. I'm not a kid anymore, so I don't expect her to be God."

And it's also permitted to let her know that your beliefs may be evolving, perhaps telling her, "I've always taught you what I thought would serve you best in life, but now I need to be free to see what might work better for myself."

For instance, one mother told me she recently informed

her teenage daughter: "A few years ago, I believed that one of the most important things I could do during the day was to get your father's dinner on the table by six. I don't see life quite that way anymore. I have other things I want and need to do. And your father is having to learn to fix some of the meals and do some other things around the house. I'm sorry if this is confusing to you, but change is what life is all about."

She can handle knowing that you have your own turmoil and confusion, because she is also going through tremendous change.

Mothers and daughters both express a need to make time for one another, emotional time and physical time. As one young girl said, "I'd like to do more simple things with my mom, like shopping or going on walks or doing projects in the house together. I guess she thinks I'm too busy or I just wouldn't be interested."

And young women have told me they do need their mothers to just *be* there, to be partners in the journey ahead. And, whether or not they are always aware of it, that's something mothers also need from their daughters.

"It's funny, there are lots of times when I don't notice my mom and all the things she does for me. And I know she does lots and lots," says small Sabrina with the large carrot-colored Afro. "But sometimes she is the only person I want to talk to, to be with. And while I don't want her to spend her life waiting around for me, I do really appreciate that when I need her I can count on her to be nearby."

Mothers need their daughters in the same way.

"Katy and I are in this thing together," says Marcy Graham. "I feel really seen by her — sometimes more than by anyone else. When I am going through a really bad time, I feel like she looks at me and thinks, 'Go ahead and rant and rave, Mom; I see who you are, anyway.' And she has told me that she is glad that I can see through all — most — of her disguises to who she really is.

"I look forward to growing up even more with her."

" 'Successful' mothers and daughters *talk* to each other," says Virginia Satir. "And they *listen* to one another. Some daughters report that they have a difficult time getting their mothers to listen — especially when the subject is something they would rather remain ignorant about."

"If I say something she's uncomfortable hearing, she goes on automatic and tunes me out," says a sixteen-year-old, with a shrug of her shoulders. "She usually does that when what I have to say crosses with her opinion, and then nobody else can be right. That bothers me a lot."

Being a good listener for your daughter obviously includes sitting down and truly paying attention — being absolutely there and nowhere else at that moment — even when you would rather be doing something else. It means strenuously avoiding preaching or interrupting; keeping quiet until she communicates all of her thoughts doesn't imply that you agree with what she is saying but merely that you accept her right to express herself.

By the same token, if it is important that you be able to communicate with her, you won't nag, laugh, be sarcastic, or accuse. ("Why did you do that?" "You should have done this.") You also need to listen to what she is saying between the words that are actually spoken. What ideas or thoughts really seem to be important to her?

When "listening" to another individual, each of us, at one time or another, tends to jump ahead and examine her own reactions and plan her replies to what the other is saying. In so doing, there is little chance that we can hear what our partner is trying to communicate. We must learn to quiet our minds — the judgmental voices — in order to listen.

And the woman whose self-esteem and security largely depend on maintaining her self-image as a better-than-good mother, with no responsibility for, or connection to, her daughter's pain or shortcomings, may have a hard time listening to her daughter's fears or anger, for she will be afraid that she will hear something about *herself* that may scar her own image.

One mother confesses that this has been a hard lesson she is still trying to learn. "I was very dependent on both my daughters to confirm me as a loving person. If they acted in a way that seemed to say they didn't feel loved, I was tremendously threatened. Of course, that put a lot of responsibility — and power — in their hands. I finally saw I had to let that go and even be seen as a bitch, if that's what it took. Sometimes I have to withstand their saying, 'I hate you,' and not try to change it."

We all need to learn reflective listening, which entails becoming a mirror for your partner in conversation. Instead of proffering a ready-made solution to her pain, it might be more helpful to simply say something like "I see that you are hurting," or "You seem to be feeling like . . . is that what is going on with you?"

Another helpful exercise in communication would start with mother and daughter sitting down together with the aim of truly attempting to understand the "other side of the story" in a situation they shared but in which each never really understood the ways it affected the other.

A daughter, then, might ask her mother: What was it like for you when I was born? When I started my first day of school? When I had my first period? When my appendix burst and I was rushed to the hospital? When I brought that scruffy-looking guy home and told you we were going steady?

In her turn, a mother may ask her daughter: What was it like for you when I got a job and left you with a full-time baby-sitter? When your father and I were going through that bad time and argued a lot? When your brother was born? When you were the star of the school Christmas pageant, and I wasn't able to come?

It is reasonable for both mother and daughter to want, to expect, to be able to have good communication with one another, but neither can always expect that communication to come in the form or the package she wants it in. Or exactly *when* she wants it.

"Some parents," says Shari Glucoft-Wong, "who used to be proud of the easy rapport they had with their kids when they were younger are now feeling angry and rejected when the answers don't come so easily now that their kids have reached adolescence.

"So they must be inventive and find new ways of connecting with their kids."

Being a good communicator may also mean being there for your daughter when she seems to be totally uninterested in communicating. She needs to know that you can be there when she is ready to talk.

If you aren't quite sure what it is your daughter needs from you — and what you are able to give her at this point in both of your lives — it might be helpful to take some time and ask yourself a few simple questions.

What purpose do I fill in her life now? Am I here to approve of her? Do I want her to be dependent on me for my opinion so that she will either live to please me or to rebel against me? Do I always want her to defer to me, simply because I am her mother? What can she learn from me? And I from her?

And remember you are giving her a gift by allowing her to know that she also can give. I heard more than one young woman express her frustration at her mother's unwillingness or inability to take from others. As one pointed out: "Instead of her being the one to give to me all the time, I would really like my mother to be able to *take* something from me, to see *me* as a giving person. I guess she has this weird idea that mothers are the ones who are supposed to do all the giving."

One of the hardest things a mother needs to do — for herself and her daughter — is to allow her daughter to grow up, even if she is afraid that this world of ours is a frightening place to be grown up in.

# 13

## *Letting Grow*

"There is a universal yearning in man for expanding his freedom, but he doesn't usually know what freedom is. So what he does is lash out blindly against limitations. . . . It is not possible to attain freedom by fighting against limitations, because freedom doesn't know limitations, and limitations are in our consciousness.

"The abundance of good is in proportion to the boundaries of the context in which we live. If we live in the context of the infinite, then infinite good is available to us."

— *Dr. Thomas Hora, Existential Metapsychiatry*

Carla Vaughn is worried about that irritating habit that history has of repeating itself.

"My first marriage was an absolute disaster," she says with a grimace. "I married at seventeen to get away from my mother, who, I felt, was holding on to me so hard I was sure I was going to break. She hated the boy I married, and that was important. In fact, I can admit it was one of the reasons I married him. Looking back, I can see that I really didn't like him much myself.

"Now that I feel my own daughter beginning to cross over some invisible line to become her own person, I realize I sometimes hold on too tightly, by worrying too much and not having enough faith. But I hope she doesn't have to go too far or throw me away entirely in order to prove something to herself, or to me, or to the world."

What is unsettling to Carla Vaughn and countless other mothers is the whole idea of "letting go" of their teenage daughters — how, when, and to what degree. While raising a child is, in reality, just one long letting go, the urges to separate become more apparent and insistent by the time adolescence comes calling.

A daughter can leave home, go away to college, get a job, get married, and have children of her own — and not really go anywhere at all, if she does not have a clear understanding of where her mother ends and she begins. While she will naturally incorporate many of her mother's values, ideas, and thoughts, growing up and separating means learning how to be selectively conscious about which of those things can work in her own life and which do not serve her.

Is letting go more or less difficult in these liberated times? The process of separation may have *seemed* less wrenching when it was generally assumed that daughters would follow placidly along in their mother's, mainly domestic, footsteps. Now, if a mother is involved in the traditional female role, and her daughter is interested in taking a more liberal route through life, a separation of ids and identities will obviously be more necessary — and quite possibly more painful.

On the other hand, for the daughter, letting go of mother's apron strings may be easier now because there are so many different kinds of female roles from which to pick and choose. If mother isn't who she wants to be like, there are other places to go, other choices to be made.

We have witnessed how some mothers try to hold on to their daughters by either attempting to mold them in their own likenesses or trying to see to it that they turn out quite differently. In fact, both of those manipulations are the same, for neither allows the young woman to be the person she needs to be. And we have seen how it is that when demands, too numerous and too persistent, are made on a young girl concerning who and what she should be, she may comply with what others want of her, without first seeing who she is and what she needs to do for herself.

We have looked at how the unreasonable expectations that mother (and daughter) usually reserve for one another are simply other ways of not letting go of our demands that life turn out the way we think it should. We need to see that our expectations have little to do with the other member of the relationship, and we all need to let go of the myth of the perfect mother and the daughter who will succeed for us in the times and the places where we have failed (or so we think) for ourselves.

But then, no one ever said that letting go of one's kids was going to be a piece of cake.

In a 1977 Gallup Youth Survey, while teenagers said they believed that the biggest problem facing their generation was drug abuse, running a close second was the array of difficulties in getting along and communicating with parents, among them being allowed to separate.

A characteristic remark from a teenager on that issue: "Our parents don't want to let us go. They think of us as children for too long. A lot of tension between kids and their parents stem from the way they hold on."

Obviously, the main stumbling block to letting go of our children — no matter what the time or place — is the degree to which we cling to the illusion that our children belong to us, that they are, in fact, ours for the having. After all, you can only lose something or someone about whom you have thoughts of possession.

The whole idea of "having" a child (including the very phrase itself) seems to reassure us that, since it was our seed and our inspiration that resulted in her appearance on the planet, and since we have housed and fed her ever since, she is ours to have. A part of letting go includes realizing we never did "have" her in the first place. The most any of us did and can do — and it is a lot — is to have an experience of who she is and a participation in life with her. All the rest is an illusion, a fairy tale.

One mother whose pride-of-ownership illusions were recently shattered says: "I remember one period when I nagged and nagged at her about the way she was eating, telling her that all these fad diets and junk food she loaded up on were no good, that she needed balanced meals, that I was tired of paying good money for nutritious food she wasn't even eating. I went on and on, especially since she never appeared to listen.

"Finally, one day she shouted at me, 'Leave me alone. I'm healthy and at a good weight. It's my life and it's none of your business.' And with a real shock, I realized, by God, that she was right."

Barbara Hayes, both mother and therapist, always had a strong sense that her daughter had a life apart from her own. "Kate, to me, has always been her own person," she says. "We have had our problems in many areas, but I don't think I ever saw her merely as an extension of me or as the person who was obligated to carry out my life or my line. I have always respected her for her individuality, and she has come to respect me for mine.

"Kate is Kate, and I have always been fascinated by her.

For me, I think it helped that I had years of my own career before I became a mom. Maybe that lent me some distance and perspective."

Another mother who learned the wisdom of beginning to let go early shares this: "When Lisa first came home from the hospital as a newborn, I commenced raising her as a separate human being. I've always seen my job as helping her find her way in the world for a few years. One way I let her know that she didn't have to *be* me, was to reassure her that the sky wouldn't fall in if she said 'no' once in a while.

"And that is very different from when I was growing up. None of the six girls in my family was ever allowed to disagree with my parents. I was the youngest, and the first one who went against them. I married too young, a man my mother didn't approve of. I got her disapproval — but I also got a little distance. Some victory."

"You just have to cut the cord and let them go," says still another mother. "You release them to do whatever they need to do in life. You can't really hold them, anyway, and the harder you try, the more it hurts everyone."

As previously mentioned, mothers still tend to hold onto and to encourage more dependency in their daughters than they do in their sons. Somehow, despite the very great inroads the feminist movement has made on our collective consciousness, when it comes right down to it, love and dependency are still dangerously synonomous for women.

Some mothers, though most are not aware of it, do seem to think that a daughter will continue to love them only as long as they need them. And so they do not applaud their daughters' independence and self-sufficiency. It is no surprise that the daughters of these women often end up living their lives as a reaction to what they think will keep the bond alive, rather than as a response to what their own intelligence or sense of what is needed asks of them.

"My mother needs to make a baby out of me, to control me," says Roxie, a quiet girl whose infant sense of self-assurance seems still so breakable. "She is dependent on me to be dependent on her. Even though she said she couldn't understand why I needed it, I have been seeing a therapist for about a year now. Mom is still pretty threatened by that, because she thinks that I am going to become dependent on my therapist instead of on her.

"Of course, my goal is to recognize that I don't have to be dependent on anyone, and that independence is not something I have to fight my mother — or anyone else — for. It is always there, ready for me when I am ready for it."

The most well-intentioned mothers may hold on to their daughters because they are genuinely frightened for them. The world seems to be offering them too many choices, and a lot of loving, well-meaning mothers want to protect their daughters from making the wrong ones.

"I have this continuing image of myself cradling Tisa in my arms and keeping the rest of the world out. I don't do that, of course. But do you realize that in the world she will be going out to face — very soon — nothing at all is guaranteed? There are no limits. I wonder if that could possibly frighten her as much as it frightens me *for* her?"

Mothers may try to hold on to their daughters in all sorts of ways, some by demanding too much, others, paradoxically, by seeming to ask nothing of them. They may be too permissive, or give their daughters far more material things than are needed, or overindulge them in other ways. All of these are forms of bribery — albeit unconscious and full of good intention — and yet they are alluring temptations for the young girl to remain a child and avoid a more demanding reality.

Sometimes, as psychologists have suggested, a woman who tries too hard to be pals with her daughter may be holding on to the only relationship she has any confidence can work. She is afraid of what having an adult daughter would tell herself and the world about who she is. But this sort of holding on can spell a lot of problems for her daughter.

"A young girl will have more trouble differentiating herself from a mother who dresses like her, who manifests other adolescent ideas, and who, in essence, is competing with her at her level," says Marilyn Mehr. "This allows for no real separation between the generations, and that is very confusing for a young girl.

"She may make it in the world, but often not too well."

Even beyond the emphasis on palship, holding on sometimes entails a reversal of roles: for all intents and purposes, mother becomes the daughter and daughter becomes the caretaker.

"Some mothers respond to the increased pressures introduced by their child's attempts to grow up by regressing into a sort of helplessness themselves, inviting a protective, solicitous response from their daughters," says Joyce Lindenbaum, a therapist in Berkeley, California.

"What amounts to a 'reversal of generations' is common and even expected when a parent becomes elderly, but now it is premature, and a teenager has a difficult time handling it. She should not be coerced into the role of therapist, nor should she be burdened with her mother's midlife problems of adjustment. Her own developmental place is too precarious to handle a parental expectation that goes something like 'Now that you are growing up, you know what I have had to go through. So stick by me; don't let me down. Don't go too far away.' "

The trade-off of mother and daughter functions is also common when a mother's relationship with her own mother was unhappy or separation was incomplete.

"If a woman has never really had the experience of being someone's daughter, in the best sense of the word, on some level she may try to turn her daughter into her mother. She may try to get her needs met in inappropriate ways, and her daughter will have a difficult time separating herself from the mother who needs her. And then we may have some real problems."

Another common means of holding on to the psychic reins is to cast a blanket of disapproval on the young girl's friends, especially her would-be boyfriends, thus putting her in the position of having to choose between her mother and the "competitors." Here a mother so unsure of herself that she can't fathom her daughter's having enough love for more than one may have a deeply subconscious thought like "I won't lose my daughter to that boy," or "If I can't have her, neither can you."

For some mothers, their daughters' struggle to find separate identities feels as if they are being rejected. And, it is true that, in searching out who she is, it often appears as if a young woman is rejecting her parents' values.

"A young girl is grasping and groping about for what she is to become," says Peggy Golden. "And what she is to become is often different from what her parents expected. In separating, she will have to leave some of their rules behind and try out some of her own rules. It is up to her parents to take none of that personally."

It would also be wise to try to remember that when your

daughter appears to reject the lessons you have tried so hard to teach her, who you are, your essence, is not being rejected. It is only the model that must be cast off, at least for a while, as she tries on other ideas of who she might be.

Parents often feel — and with obvious justification — that their teenage kids are not respectful enough of them, but in the process of separating, some degree of rebellion is natural. And, by its nature, rebellion does not imply respect. While parents needn't take a lot of guff, they might as well come to expect less docile, obedient behavior and to realize that at least some of a daughter's negativity toward her parents is one way of proving — probably before she really believes it herself — that she doesn't need them the way she used to.

"I have gone through being yelled at, misunderstood, and ignored with my two older children," says psychologist Sandy Rader. "I assume my youngest will do the same thing. It just seems to be part of the process. It can be very painful for me, and, believe me, I don't like being hurt, but I also recognize that they may sometimes need to say 'no' to me, in order to learn how to say 'yes' to themselves. It's their way of cutting the ties.

"But underneath the unpleasantness, there is a bond. My oldest — she's nineteen — can walk away and not call me for a month at a time because she knows I'll be there — I always have been — when she wants to come back. I work with disturbed adolescents, and many of their mothers have never really been there for them. They need to call their mothers every day. They cry for them every night. It will take a lot of work for those kids ever to be able to see themselves as separate from the image they hold of their mothers."

Nan, sixteen, understands that her adolescence and her

attempts to grow up out of it are not always easy for her mother. "I don't want to get married early and just be a wife and a mother, which is what my mother did with her life," says the would-be biochemist. "But I am definitely not rejecting the things my mother stands for — the honesty, the generosity, the strength, the humor. In those ways, I only hope I can turn out to be at least a little bit like her."

Young women are themselves not always one hundred percent sure that growing up and separating from Mom is the world's best idea. I remember, not many years back, making statements — sometimes in words, sometimes in actions that spoke louder — that told my mother, "I'm free. And that means I am me, not you. Let go of me."

In the very next breath, I was saying, "I'm scared. Hold me tight."

I wanted separation, and I wanted to mend the rip that had been made in the umbilical cord so many years before. "Give me your written permission to pack up who I am and leave this house — but if you love me like you say you do, you won't let me go."

"The fear of losing Mother altogether, if we separate our identity from hers, can result in tremendous anger or depression or both," says Vivian Kaplan. "We are often afraid we will be completely alone if we don't stay close to her or carry her around inside of us."

Some girls think that fleeing home altogether might be an easier method of separation than the gradual — endless — psychic rips and tears, but find that Mother is not so easy to get rid of. "When I ran away from home, it was more scary to me that I was doing something against my mother than it was to be out on the street with no food or money or a place to live," says scrawny, feisty Cynthia. "I have such a hard time being with her, but there is no way I know of to get away from her. She is with me in everything I do or think. Everything boils down to 'Will she still love me, approve of me?' "

In their own ambivalence, our daughters don't always make it easy for us to know just how much separation and independence they really want. They may alternately take very deliberate stands to show us just how liberated they are, and then turn around and do something else to suggest they need us to take care of them. They want freedom and, at the same time, they want safety, and they believe those things to be mutually exclusive.

"Katy is very ambivalent about wanting to grow up," says Marcie Graham. "Sometimes I give her extra responsibility, and she promptly screws up the opportunity. For instance, we recently made plans for the whole family to go away for the weekend, but Katy asked to be allowed to stay home alone. After thinking about it carefully, we felt that she might be ready for it.

"We left her money for food and emergencies and whatever. She lost the money. She forgot to pick up her cousin from a doctor's appointment. And she got in a minor accident with the car.

"It seems very obvious to my husband and to me that she was pulling back from the responsibility she said she wanted by being as careless as she used to be when she was a little girl."

In such cases, where it is unclear what is really needed, Edith Kasin advises "standing back, but standing by. If you can get past your own need for approval from her and your concern about whether you have been a good mother, you can hear her tell you quite plainly just how much freedom she is ready for."

The fact that this just happens to be a time of crisis of identity in your life certainly does not make it any easier to let go. For all practical purposes, your career as a mother is coming to a close. You may not only feel called upon to resolve your relationsip with your daughter, but you may be poignantly aware of the unfinished business you have with your own parents, who, if they are not already, may soon be elderly and dependent on you.

Whether you have been a working woman or a home-maker, when you hit forty or thereabouts, you begin to ask yourself questions that may have disturbing answers for you: What has my life been about? Has my marriage been fulfilling? Have I done any, some, all of the things I used to dream of? And is there time enough left to do those things?

You may be alternately glad for the freedom to spend less time in caring for your children and sad that you aren't needed in quite the same ways anymore. One moment you may find yourself issuing a silent prayer that your daughter be allowed to remain your little girl for just a little while longer, and shortly thereafter get so exasperated at her that you wish to heaven she would go far, far away for a long, long time.

"Many women are glad that their children are growing up, glad that they can get back to being themselves again or becoming once more part of the couple they used to be," says Edith Kasin. "Husband and wife may now see themselves as freer to turn to one another, although, of course, that freedom was always there, even though they may have chosen to ignore it.

"For some, this new time together can be filled with joy and renewal. For others, it can bring to the forefront problems that may have been brewing unchecked for years."

And that brings up an important issue: the woman who has ignored the other-than-motherly dimensions of her self-image and identity may well have a much tougher time letting her daughter separate and grow up. She may even see her daughter's attempt to become her own person as a sign of ingratitude or as a threat to her own self-concept.

"The mothers who feel they have nothing but their 'motherness' tend to hold on to their daughters," says Vivian Kaplan, "and the woman whose whole life has been predicated on being a model mother needs to have a model child. And then we are in for some trouble."

Thus, if a woman has seen herself only as a mother who has lived her life in the service of her children, the hole will seem much deeper and harder to fill when her children leave. She will be more likely to be left depressed, ungratified, and frustrated. Such a predicament brings to mind those "senior citizens" who simply give up and die, physically or spiritually, shortly after they retire, because they also fail to see their own value outside the work they do.

"At this point in my life, if Marissa walked out the door, I would be a lonely lady," says Gina Molino with simple poignance. "I want to be able to let her go and say, '*Buona fortuna,* I wish you luck,' and mean it. It is important that I am just as whole and complete after she walks out the door."

If you see yourself as your own person, making a unique contribution to life, then you no longer think of how your children's behavior is a reflection on you. You will be aware of other things which reflect just as truly who you are.

"I have things I want to do for myself," says Gina Molino. "I want to go back to school, to travel, to start my own business, maybe to find a loving man I can share it all with. Marissa is not the only one who wants to grow."

Of course, it's better if you don't wait until your children are grown to cultivate other interests. If you do, you've deprived them of knowing a part of you. And, if your daughter feels as if you have devoted your entire life to her, she may feel there is no way she can ever repay you or appropriately show her appreciation, and she may feel tremendous guilt when — if — she tries to separate.

All in all, it is also much easier for your young woman to have a sense of her mother as a separate person if you have something of your own going, something that really has nothing to do with her. And it's not so much being a so-called liberated woman with a career that is important as it is to be conscious about *who* you are and what you stand for.

"I have had to figure out different ways of starting over," says one mother who is trying to do that. "That has included seeking freedom from my old ideas of who I always thought I was. I do feel more free than I ever have — more free in my marriage, more free to go back to school and learn some new things, more free to make new commitments to growth and to finding out who else I am besides a loving and loved wife and mother."

Letting her go means so many things. It may include relinquishing the idea that you can — or even have a right to — wipe away all of her hurts. And that is not always so easy, for there seems to be so *much* hurting during adolescence. More than a few mothers still hold to the idea that it is part of their job to empathize so strongly with their daughters that they can almost absorb their pain.

But letting go of your need to experience her pain frees her to become less interested in where it hurts, and frees you to become more interested in the individual underneath the pain.

For both mother and daughter, letting go also means letting go of the guilt: a mother's guilt for having been imperfect, a daughter's guilt at having within her grasp that which was unavailable to her mother. Keeping up the guilt is a very good way of clinging, and it doesn't seem to matter that what is being clung to is illusory.

Letting go means forgiving the flaws in one another. And, whether or not we are quite ready to let go of the notion that all of our weaknesses are a legacy from Mother, those of us who are daughters, at fourteen or forty, might be advised to give her a little credit for what is strong, creative, lovely, and whole within us.

Letting go also includes the realization, and acceptance, that we may share less of our daughter's world than we did before. She may prefer to be with her friends more than she does with us. She may be less excited than she once was about going on family outings or vacations. She may have new secrets, which she now shares with others.

Letting go means letting her be, not what you want or need her to be, but what she is — even if that seems to be very different from who you are. It involves recognizing her uniqueness, and believing in her vision of life, even if it is not your vision.

Many parents today — parents who have beautiful, loving, but not particularly ambitious daughters — fail to see them as having turned out as well as they expected and as the "unlimited" opportunities might allow. The woman who is disappointed her daughter wants to be a beautician instead of a nuclear physicist needs to learn to choose what her daughter has chosen for herself.

"I need my mother to let me know I'm OK," says a young girl with quiet urgency. "I really need to *hear* her say it. I need her to look at where I'm coming from and where I want to go, not where she wants me to end up."

But mothers need the same sort of encouragement from their daughters. "It isn't that I need her approval to start my own business. After all, I am an adult and she isn't — quite — yet. But I would like some acknowledgment from her for my efforts or maybe an extra hug once in a while. She isn't the only one who is trying to grow up. It's just that in my case, it's the second time around."

For a young woman, letting go means beginning to take responsibility for her own life, to be neither disappointed nor resentful when her mother no longer tries to protect her from life's hurts. Only when she can abandon the idea that her mother is supposed to make sure she gets everything she wants and needs can she even begin to look to herself and to life itself as the source of real joy and aliveness.

You can help her if you can let those ideas loose first, including the idea that she needs to seek your approval for everything she does. If you don't, she will have a very tough time functioning well without the approval of others who may become important to her. And if she can't recognize her independence from you, she will go through life trying to prove her independence from others, continually suspecting that they are interested in snatching away her autonomy.

"If your daughter has never experienced a real differentiation between who you are and who she is, it is very likely that that conflict will have to be worked out in her marriage," says Barbara Hayes. "And especially if both partners in the marriage are struggling for freedom and independence, as is so often the case these days, the prognosis for the marriage is not very good."

Often the girls who have the most difficult times separating are the daughters of women who are still clinging in some way to *their* mothers. And that may account for a large number of the tightly knotted apron strings in the world, which does not mean we are suffering from chronic immaturity, if at thirty-five or forty or eighty, we find ourselves looking toward others to lean on once in a while.

" 'Letting go' is not a process many of us fully complete when we are still teenagers," Fern Rubin reassures us. "I still have unresolved dependence. It's just that most of the time I am no longer foolish enough to look toward my parents to help me resolve them. But I most certainly still look toward others in my life to help me work those things out."

The absolute, only way you can continue to have a relationship with your daughter that is perennially flowering and growing is to let her go, to help her separate her image from yours, and to see yourself as a separate being. Then a *real* friendship can blossom — different from the sort that is invented when Mother, especially, is uncomfortable with her ideas about what the maternal role should be, and so tries to abdicate by becoming a bosom buddy.

Finally, these two individuals called mother and daughter, individuals who are separate but unalterably connected through a bond of love, find they no longer have to clutch tightly the past or put a mortgage on the future. They can acknowledge and appreciate their common interests, and can take pleasure in one another, both in the ways in which they are alike and the ways they are different.

But to get there, you first must give up all of your old ideas that this child belongs to you, and when you *know* that *your* daughter is not *your* problem, which you alone can handle, you will find it far easier simply to love her. The instant you truly recognize that she can take care of herself, and that life will fully support her in that endeavor, both of you will be far along the freedom road.

You have come a very long way indeed, Mother. You started out with a babe who was totally dependent on you for survival and, you can hope, you are going to end up with a human being who is dependent on you for no *thing*.

And then the only reason left for you to *be* together, to keep the connection going, is the love that has always been there.

# Bibliography

Abelson, Herbert I., et al. *National Survey on Drug Abuse: 1977: A Nationwide Study — Youth, Young Adults and Older People.* Social Research Group, George Washington University. Rockville, Md.: National Institute on Drug Abuse, 1977.

"Abolishing Sex Stereotypes in Education." *Los Angeles Times,* September 24, 1978.

Allen, Jill. "Identity Formation in Late-Adolescent Women." Ph.D. dissertation, City University of New York, 1976.

"Anorexia Nervosa: A Diet Disease That Proves Thin Is Dangerous." *New York Times,* May 11, 1978.

Anthony, E. James. "The Reaction of Adults to Adolescents and Their Behavior." *Contemporary Issues in Adolescent Development,* ed. John Janeway Conger. New York: Harper and Row, 1975.

Arehart-Treichel, Joan. "America's Teen Pregnancy Epidemic." *Science News,* May 6, 1978.

Babst, Dean V., et al. "A Study of Family Affinity and Substance Use." *Journal of Drug Education,* 8(1): 29–40, 1978.

Baizerman, Michael. "Can the First Pregnancy of a Young Adolescent Be Prevented? A Question Which Must Be Answered." *Journal of Youth and Adolescence,* 6(4), 1977.

———, et al. *Pregnant Adolescents: A Review of Litterature With Abstracts 1960–1970.* Pittsburgh: Graduate School of Public Health, University of Pittsburgh, 1976.

Barclay, Delores. "Parenthood in Adolescence." *Los Angeles Times,* July 10, 1977.

Berger, Gertrude. "Females and Social Occupations: Forced or Free Choice." *The School Counselor,* March 1978.

Berman, Laura. "Mothers Influence Sexual Behavior." *Long Beach Independent, Press-Telegram,* July 29, 1979.

Beyette, Beverly. "A Mother-Daughter Day of Dialogue." *Los Angeles Times,* May 15, 1979.

Blau, Rita. "The Pregnant Teenager and Her Mother." Ph.D. dissertation, California School of Professional Psychology, 1978.

Brozan, Nadine. "A New Survey of Teenage Sex — With Teenagers Asking the Questions." *New York Times,* February 25, 1978.

Bruch, Hilde. *The Golden Cage: The Enigma of Anorexia Nervosa.* Cambridge: Harvard University Press, 1978.

Cantor, Pamela C. "Personality Characteristics Found among Youthful Female Suicide Attempters." *Journal of Abnormal Psychology,* 85(3), 1976.

Card, Josefina J. *Consequences of Adolescent Childbearing For the Young Parents' Future Personal and Professional Life.* Palo Alto: American Institutes for Research, 1977.

————. *Long-Term Consequences for Children Born to Adolescent Parents.* Palo Alto: American Institutes for Research, 1978.

————, and Lauress L. Wise. "Teenage Mothers and Teenage Fathers: The Impact of Early Childbearing on the Parents' Personal and Professional Lives." *Family Planning Perspectives,* 10(4), July/August 1978.

Card, Josefina J. and Richard V. Carter. *Teenage Parenthood May Be Dangerous to Your Well-Being.* Palo Alto: American Institutes for Research, 1978.

Castleman, Michael. "Why Teenagers Get Pregnant." *The Nation,* November 26, 1977.

Chase-Marshall, Janet. "Teenage Suicide." *Good Housekeeping,* May 1979.

Chesney-Lind, Meda. "Judicial Paternalism and the Female Status Offender: Training Women to Know Their Place." *Crime and Delinquency,* April 1977.

Clark, Matt. "Slow Motion Suicide." *Newsweek,* January 22, 1979.

Comfort, Alex. *The Joy of Sex: A Gourmet Guide to Lovemaking.* New York: Simon and Schuster, 1972.

Conway, Allan, and Carol Bogdan. "Sexual Delinquency: The Persistence of a Double Standard." *Crime and Delinquency,* April 1977.

Cox, Sue, et al. *Female Psychology: The Emerging Self.* Chicago: Science Research Associates, 1976.

Crook, Thomas, and Allen Raskin. "Association of Childhood Parental Loss with Attempted Suicide and Depression." *Journal of Consulting and Clinical Psychology,* 43(2), 1975.

Cvetkovich, George, et al. "Sex Role Development and Teenage Fertility-Related Behavior." *Adolescence,* 13(50), Summer 1978.

Department of Health, Education and Welfare, Center for Disease Control. *Teenage Fertility in the United States.* Washington, D.C., 1978.

Dryfoos, Joy G., and Toni Heisler. "Contraceptive Services for Adolescents: An Overview." *Family Planning Perspectives,* 10(4), July/August, 1978.

Duke, Daniel Linden. "Why Don't Girls Misbehave More than Boys in School?" *Journal of Youth and Adolescence*, 7(2), 1978.

*Eleven Million Teenagers: What Can Be Done About the Epidemic of Adolescent Pregnancies in the United States.* New York: The Alan Guttmacher Institute, Planned Parenthood Federation of America, 1976.
Elkind, David. "Egocentrism in Adolescence." *Contemporary Issues in Adolescent Development*, ed. John Janeway Conger, New York: Harper and Row, 1975.
———. "Growing up Faster." *Psychology Today*, February 1979.
Erikson, Erik W. *Identity: Youth and Crisis.* New York: Norton, 1968.
Ewer, Phyllis A., and James O. Gibbs. "School Return Among Pregnant Adolescents." *Journal of Youth and Adolescence*, 5(2), 1976.

Fadem, Susan. "Exploring the Mother-Daughter Bond." *Los Angeles Times*, July 31, 1977.
Faunce, Patricia S. "Psychological Barriers to Occupational Success for Women." *Journal of the National Association for Women Deans, Administrators, and Counselors*, Summer 1977.
Ferguson, Patricia, et al. *Drugs and Family/Peer Influence: Family and Peer Influences on Adolescent Drug Use.* Rockville, Md.: National Institute on Drug Abuse, 1974.
Finn, Peter. "Should Alcohol Education Be Taught with Drug Education?" *The Journal of School Health*, October 1977.
Fosburgh, Lacey. "The Make-Believe World of Teenage Maternity." *New York Times*, August 7, 1977.
Frederick, Calvin J. "Three-Quarters of a Century of Suicide Data in the United States." Unpublished paper presented at the Thirteenth National Scientific Meeting of the Association for the Advancement of Psychotherapy, May 1977.
———. *Trends in Mental Health: Self-Destructive Behavior Among Younger Age Groups.* Rockville, Md: Department of Health, Education and Welfare; Alcohol, Drug Abuse and Mental Health Administration, 1976.
Freeman, Ellen W. "Abortion: Subjective Attitudes and Feelings." *Family Planning Perspectives*, 10(3), May/June 1978.
Friday, Nancy. *My Mother/My Self: The Daughter's Search for Identity*, New York: Delacorte Press, 1977.
Fox, Vivian C. "Is Adolescence a Phenomenon of Modern Times?" *The Journal of Psychohistory*, Fall 1977.

Galisky, Anne. "It's a Hide-and-Seek World for the Teens of the Watergate Generation," *Los Angeles Times*, May 28, 1979.
Gamarekian, Barbara. "Two Well-Known Clubs for Girls Evolve to Meet New Needs." *New York Times*, December 24, 1977.
Gaskell, Jane. "Sex-Role Ideology and the Aspirations of High School Girls." *Interchange*, 8(3), 1977–1978.

Geyer, Georgie Anne. "Boys Want Sex, Girls Romance." *Los Angeles Times*, January 22, 1978.
———. "For Teens, Sexual Ignorance is Rarely Bliss." *Los Angeles Times*, January 22, 1978.
Gibbons, Patricia A., and Richard E. Kopelman. "Maternal Employment as a Determinant of Success in Females." *Psychological Reports*, vol. 40, 1977.
Green, Cynthia P., and Susan J. Lowe. "Teenage Pregnancy: A Major Problem for Minors." *Current*, April, 1977.
Greve, Frank. "Teen Pregnancy Crisis Defies Standard Curbs." *Long Beach Independent Press-Telegram*, May 26, 1978.

Hart, Nancy Ann. "How Teachers Can Help Suicidal Adolescents." *The Clearinghouse*, April 1978.
Hendrix, Kathleen. "The Responsibilities of Teen Fathers." *Los Angeles Times*, January 17, 1979.
Hetherington, E. Mavis. "Effects of Father Absence on Personality Development in Adolescent Daughters." *Contemporary Issues in Adolescent Development*, ed. John Janeway Conger. New York: Harper and Row, 1975.
Hickey, William. "Status Offenses and the Juvenile Court." *Criminal Justice Abstracts*, March 1977.
Hines, William. "Teenage Pregnancies: An Epidemic Increase." *Los Angeles Times*, March 19, 1978.
Hopkins, J. Roy. "Sexual Behavior in Adolescence." *Journal of Social Issues*, 33(2), 1977.
Hora, Thomas. *Dialogues in Metapsychiatry.* New York: The Seabury Press, 1977.
———. *Existential Metapsychiatry.* New York: The Seabury Press, 1977.
———. *In Quest of Wholeness: Essays and Dialogues.* Garden Grove, Calif.: Christian Counseling Service, 1972.
Horner, Matina. "The Motive to Avoid Success and Changing Aspirations of College Women." *Contemporary Issues in Adolescent Development*, ed. John Janeway Conger. New York: Harper and Row, 1975.
Howard, Maureen. "Charting Life With a Daughter." *New York Times*, June 1, 1977.
Hurowitz, Laurie, and Eugene L. Gaier. "Adolescent Erotica and Female Self-Concept Development." *Adolescence*, 11(44), Winter 1976.

Jekel, James F. "Primary or Secondary Prevention of Adolescent Pregnancies." *The Journal of School Health*, October 1977.
Johnston, Lloyd D., et al. *Drug Use Among American High School Students, 1975–1977.* Institute for Social Research, University of Michigan. Rockville, Md.: National Institute on Drug Abuse, 1978.
Jolly, Mary Kaaren. "Female Delinquency: National Policies and Priorities." Paper presented at the National Conference: Changing Values:

Teenage Women in the Juvenile Justice System. Tucson, Arizona, November 5, 1977.

Jones, Priscilla S. "Parenthood Education in a City High School." *Children Today* (Department of Health, Education and Welfare), March-April 1975.

Josselson, Ruthellen. "Phenomenological Aspects of Psychosocial Maturity in Adolescence. Part II. Girls." *Journal of Youth and Adolescence*, 6(2), 1977.

Kay, Jane. "Juvenile Injustice: Experts Find Courts Guilty in Treatment of Female Young." *Arizona Daily Star*, November 7, 1977.

Keniston, Kenneth. "Should We Stop Blaming Parents?" *New York Times*, October 19, 1977.

Kitwood, Tom M. "On Values and Value-Systems: Evidence from Interviews With Adolescents." *Educational Research*, June 1976.

Klagsbrun, Francine. "How to Prevent Teenage Suicide." *Seventeen*, October 1976.

Konner, Melvin J. "Adolescent Pregnancy." *New York Times*, September 24, 1977.

Kreider, Douglas G., and Jerome A. Motto. "Parent-Child Role Reversal and Suicidal States in Adolescence." *Adolescence*, 9(35), Fall 1974.

Lasch, Christopher. *The Culture of Narcissism: American Life in an Age of Diminishing Expectations*. New York: W. W. Norton and Co., 1979.

Lavach, John F., and Hope B. Lanier. "The Motive to Avoid Success in High-Achieving Girls, Grades 7–12." *Phi Delta Kappan*, December 1976.

Lee, Essie E. "Female Adolescent Drinking Behavior: Potential Hazards." *Journal of School Health*, March 1978.

Lettieri, Dan J. Predicting Adolescent Drug Abuse: A Review of Issues, Methods and Correlates. Rockville, Md.: National Institute on Drug Abuse, 1974.

"Lib-Alcoholism Link Explored." *Los Angeles Times*, June 6, 1979.

Liddick, Betty. "Teen Health Going Up in Smoke?" *Los Angeles Times*, February 24, 1978.

Lobsenz, Dorothea Harding. "What You Wish Your Teenager Never Told You about Sex." *Ms.*, May 1975.

"Majority of Americans Favor Legal Abortion, Sex Education and Contraceptive Services for Teens." *Family Planning Perspectives*, 10(3), May/June 1978.

Markham, Margaret, and Howard Jacobson. "Unwed Teenage Mothers." *Parents Magazine*, June 1976.

Marini, Margaret Mooney, and Ellen Greenberger. "Sex Differences in Educational Aspirations and Expectations." *American Educational Research Journal*, 15(1), Winter 1978.

Mayes, Bea. "Women, Equality, and the Public High School." *Education*, 97(4).

Miller, John P. "Suicide and Adolescence." *Adolescence*, 10(37), Spring 1975.

Miller, Thomas W. "The Effects of Core Facilitative Conditions in Mother on Adolescent Self-Esteem." *The Journal of Social Psychology*, vol. 100, 1976.

Milton, Catherine. *Little Sisters and the Law*. Washington: Female Offender Resource Center. American Bar Association. 1977.

Minuchin, Salvador, et al. *Psychosomatic Families: Anorexia Nervosa in Context*. Cambridge: Harvard University Press, 1978.

"Mounting a Counterattack against Child Alcoholism." *U.S. News and World Report*, July 11, 1977.

National Family Planning Forum. *Planned Births, The Future of the Family and the Quality of American Life*. New York: Alan Guttmacher Institute, 1977.

National Institute on Alcohol Abuse and Alcoholism. *Alcohol and Health: Second Special Report to the U.S. Congress*. Rockville, Md., 1975.

――――. *The Drinking Question: Honest Answers to Questions Teenagers Ask about Drinking*. Rockville, Md., 1979.

National Organization for Non-Parents. *Am I Parent Material?* Baltimore.

Planned Parenthood Center of Syracuse, Inc. *Sex Education at Home*. Syracuse, N.Y., 1974.

"Need Cited to Help Teenage Mothers." *Los Angeles Times*, December 19, 1977.

Nelson, Harry. "Children are Adults' Pawns." *Los Angeles Times*, January 17, 1979.

――――. "Rapid Rise in Teen Drug Use in Last Ten Years Found." *Los Angeles Times*, March 30, 1977.

Nordheimer, Jon. "The Family in Transition: A Challenge From Within." *New York Times*, November 27, 1977.

"Number of Children in Divorces Triples." *Los Angeles Times*, July 2, 1979.

Nye, F. Ivan. *School-Age Parenthood*. Ames: Iowa State University Press, 1978.

Offit, Avodan K. "Anxiety: Offspring of Sexual Revolution." *Los Angeles Times*, December 4, 1977.

Paton, Stephanie M., and Denise B. Kardel. "Psychological Factors and Adolescent Illicit Drug Use: Ethnicity and Sex Differences." *Adolescence*, 13(50), Summer 1978.

Peacock, Carol. *Program for Female Juvenile Offenders: Phase II*. Boston: Department of Youth Services, Commonwealth of Massachusetts, December, 1977.

Peck, Michael L. "Suicide Motivation in Adolescents." *Adolescence*, 3(9), Spring 1968.

――――, and Robert E. Litman. *Current Trends in Youthful Suicide*. Los

Angeles: The Institute for Studies of Destructive Behaviors and the Suicide Prevention Center, 1975.

Peterson, Anne C. "Can Puberty Come Any Earlier? *Psychology Today,* February 1979.

Planned Parenthood Federation of New York. *How to Talk to Your Teenages About Something that's Not Easy to Talk About.* New York.

Poole, Carol. "Contraception and the Adolescent Female." *Journal of School Health,* October 1976.

Potter, Sandra J., and Herbert L. Smith. "Sex Education as Viewed by Teenage Unwed Mothers." *Intellect,* April 1976.

"Pregnant Teens." *Newsweek,* May 30, 1977.

Putzel, Michael. "Teen Pregnancy Study Says Abortion Essential." *Long Beach Independent Press-Telegram.* November 28, 1979.

Query, Joy M. N., and Thomas C. Kuruville. "Male and Female Adolescent Achievement and Maternal Employment." *Adolescence,* 10(39), Fall 1975.

Reinhold, Robert. "Birth Rate Among Girls 15 to 17 Rises in 'Puzzling' 10-Year Trend." *New York Times,* September 21, 1977.

———. "The Trend Toward Sexual Equality: Depth of Transformation Uncertain." *New York Times,* November 30, 1977.

Rich, Adrienne. *Of Woman Born: Motherhood as Experience and Institution.* New York: W. W. Norton & Co., 1976.

Roberts, Steven V. "The Epidemic of Teenage Pregnancy." *New York Times,* June 18, 1978.

Rosenkrantz, Arthur L. "A Note on Adolescent Suicide: Incidence, Dynamics and Some Suggestions for Treatment." *Adolescence,* 13(50), Summer 1978.

Rubin, Nancy. "Sex and the Teenager (For Parents)." *New York Times,* May 21, 1978.

Rutter, Michael, et al. "Adolescent Turmoil: Fact or Fiction?" *Journal of Child Psychology and Psychiatry,* vol. 17, 1976.

Ryerson, William. *Program to Expand Sexuality Education in Cooperation With Youth Serving Agencies, Progress Report: July-December 1978.* Washington, D.C.: The Population Institute, 1978.

Sarri, Rosemary, and Yeheskel Hasenfeld. *Brought to Justice? Juveniles, The Courts and the Law.* Ann Arbor: National Assessment of Juvenile Corrections, August 1976.

Satir, Virginia. *Peoplemaking.* Palo Alto: Science and Behavior Books, 1972.

Scales, Peter. "Males and Morals: Teenage Contraceptive Behavior Amid the Double Standard." *The Family Coordinator,* July 1977.

Scarf, Maggie. "The More Sorrowful Sex." *Psychology Today,* April 1979.

Schippers, Louis. "The Permanence of Change and the Adolescent Experience." *Adolescence,* 13(49), Spring 1978.

Schultz, Terri. "The Feelings Too Many Daughters Are Afraid to Face." *Redbook*, October 1976.

"Sexes Equal in Alcohol and Drug Use." *Science News*, April 30, 1977.

Smith, Dave. "Help for Children with Own Children." *Los Angeles Times*, November 8, 1978.

"Smoking in Children and Adolescents — Psychosocial Determinants and Prevention Strategies." *Smoking and Health: a Report of the Surgeon General*. Washington, D.C.: Department of Health, Education, and Welfare, 1979.

Snider, Arthur J. "Sex as a Teenage Cry for Help." *Los Angeles Times*, May 7, 1978.

Stix, Harriet. "The Problem of Losing Too Much Weight." *Los Angeles Times*, July 23, 1975.

Sugar, Max. "At-Risk Factors for the Adolescent Mother and Her Infant." *Journal of Youth and Adolescence*, 5(3), 1976.

Swanson, Jon Colby. "Junior High Student Evaluations of Drug Education by Values and Traditional Oriented Teachers." *Journal of Drug Education*, Spring 1974.

"Teenage Drinking." *Business Week*, March 6, 1978.

Teicher, Joseph D. "A Solution to the Chronic Problem of Living: Adolescent Attempted Suicide." Los Angeles: unpublished paper.

————. "Children and Adolescents Who Attempt Suicide." *Pediatric Clinics of North America*, 17(3), August 1970.

Tietze, Christopher. "Teenage Pregnancies: Looking Ahead to 1984." *Family Planning Perspectives*, 10(4), July/August 1978.

Timnick, Lois. "Is Turn-on Turning Off in California?" *Los Angeles Times*, December 28, 1978.

Tooley, Kay M. "The Remembrance of Things Past." *American Journal of Orthopsychiatry*, January 1978.

"Trouble in an Affluent Suburb: Teenage Suicides Galvanize a New Jersey Community." *Time*, December 25, 1978.

Trussell, James, and Jane Menken. "Early Childbearing and Subsequent Fertility." *Family Planning Perspectives*, 10(4), July/August 1978.

Van Gelder, Laurence. "Despite Feminism, Americans Still Prefer a Son to a Daughter." *New York Times*, January 29, 1978.

Vils, Ursula. "Treating Teens Who Starve for Thinness' Sake." *Los Angeles Times*, October 22, 1978.

Wagner, Hilmar. "The Adolescent and His Religion." *Adolescence*, 13(50), Summer 1978.

Waterman, Caroline K., and Jeffrey S. Nevid. "Sex Differences in the Resolution of the Identity Crisis." *Journal of Youth and Adolescence*, 6(4), 1977.

Wechsler, Henry, and Mary McFadden. "Sex Differences in Adolescent Alcohol and Drug Use: A Disappearing Phenomenon." *Journal of Studies on Alcohol*, 37(9), 1976.

Wedemeyer, Dee. "For Teenagers, A Different Kind of Sex Education." *New York Times*, March 10, 1977.

Yarro, Barbara. "American Youth: Too Much Too Soon?" *Los Angeles Times*, September 21, 1979.

Zelnik, Melvin, and John F. Kanter. "Contraceptive Patterns and Premarital Pregnancy Among Women Aged 15–19 in 1976." *Family Planning Perspectives*, 10(3), May/June 1978.

———. "Sexual and Contraceptive Experience of Young Unmarried Women in the United States, 1976 and 1971." *Family Planning Perspectives*, 9(2), March/April 1977.

Zey-Ferrell, Mary, et al. "The Intergenerational Socialization of Sex-Role Attitudes: A Gender or Generational Gap?" *Adolescence*, 13(49), Spring 1978.

Zongker, Calvin E. "The Self-Concept of Pregnant Adolescent Girls." *Adolescence*, 12(48), Winter 1977.

# *Author's Acknowledgments*

THERE ARE SO MANY other people who, in one way or another, helped me with this book. In no special order, they include Joe Bell, who was first my excellent and inspiring writing teacher, then my ever-interested mentor, and, finally, an abiding friend and colleague. Dick McDonough — a perceptive and creative editor is a joy to have, but one who cares to understand the person behind the writer must be a gift from above. Vivian Lichter Kaplan, who so many years ago believed in miracles and helped one to bloom.

Fern Rubin — teacher, counselor, mother of teenage daughters, friend and spiritual presence — who was willing to be whichever of those was needed most whenever I asked. Jan Linthorst and Thomas Hora, teachers of Real Life. My agent, Barbara Lowenstein, who "nudged" me out of my limited view of myself as a magazine writer and who kept on nudging until this book was finally finished.

My many dear friends who were there for me when a difficult personal time in my life interrupted my work — especially to Cynthia Whitcomb Mandelberg, who lovingly helped me "get off it," more than once, and Donna Barden Evans, whose deep caring and abiding faith kept reminding me that someone with much broader shoulders than mine was always there to bear the burden. To Ilene, Steve, Chris, Betty, Teri, Ben, and all the others who have helped me to see that love is limitless.

To Barbara Hunt and Joy Lazo, who transcribed hour upon hour of interview tapes, and Lucile Jagerson, who sometimes had to decipher hieroglyphics to type this manuscript.

To the many mothers and daughters who shared their stories with me and taught me so much, and who then were often kind enough to thank me for helping them learn things about themselves they hadn't known before. That was one of the most gratifying aspects of the entire project.

I am deeply grateful to the following professionals who shared their time, expertise, and compassion:

Rita Blau, Ph.D.: clinical psychologist, division of adolescent medicine, Children's Hospital of Los Angeles; author of a dissertation on the relationship between the pregnant teenager and her mother

John Bolf, Ph.D.: psychologist and director of the adolescent substance abuse program at Care Manor Hospital, Tustin, California

Peter Chambers, M.A.: therapist with troubled and addicted teenagers at Care Manor Hospital

Maurie C. Cullen, M.S.S.S.: licensed clinical social worker, Western Psychological Center, Encino, California; teacher of teenage sexuality and parent-teenager relationships at the Center for the Improvement of Child Caring, Los Angeles, California

Jacqueline Ficht, R.N.: nurse practitioner; counsels young women on sexuality, pregnancy, and drug abuse, division of adolescent medicine, Children's Hospital of Los Angeles

Shari Glucoft-Wong: marriage, family, and child counselor, Institute of Human Development, Berkeley, California

Peggy Golden: sex therapist and educator and family planning consultant, with UCLA's Human Sexuality Program and in private practice; mother of a teenage daughter

Barbara Hayes, M.A.: marriage, family, and child counselor; former actress, who, with Sherry Mandan, teaches creative communication training for mothers and daughters of all ages; mother of a teenage daughter

Robert Iles, D.D.: licensed marriage, family, and child counselor, Pasadena, California; teacher of human sexuality at Santa Monica College; Episcopal priest

Vivian Kaplan, M.A.: clinical psychologist, Highland Park, Illinois. Has worked extensively with anorexic girls and other troubled adolescents and their families

Edith Kasin: licensed marriage, family, and child counselor, Berkeley, California. With Joyce Lindenbaum, has led many mother-daughter workshops, in addition to group and private counseling with mother-daughter pairs

Joyce Lindenbaum: licensed marriage, family, and child counselor, Berkeley (See Edith Kasin)

Linda Lowrey: registered nurse and nurse practitioner; in charge of counseling program for pregnant adolescents and teenage mothers, Hollywood-Presbyterian Hospital

Sherry Mandan, M.A.: licensed marriage, family, and child counselor (see Barbara Hayes)

Marilyn Mehr, Ph.D.: clinical psychologist; coordinator, psychosocial services, division of adolescent medicine, Children's Hospital of Los Angeles

Pat Mitchell: director and counselor, OK Corral, residential treatment center for teenage drug and alcohol abusers, Orange County, California; mother of a teenage daughter

Donald Orr, M.D.: division of adolescent medicine, University of California at Irvine Medical Center

Maria Piers, Ph.D.: Distinguished Service Professor, therapist, Erik Erikson Institute for Early Education, Chicago, Illinois

Sandy Rader, Ph.D.: clinical psychologist and therapist with schizophrenic adolescents; mother of two teenage daughters and a teenage son

Fern Rubin, M.S.: licensed marriage, family, and child counselor; teaches classes on human sexuality and on aging; mother of two teenage daughters

Lucie L. Rudd, M.D.: director, adolescent medicine, Roosevelt Hospital, New York, New York

Virginia Satir: teacher, therapist, trainer in family communications; one of the founders of family therapy; widely published author, including two "bibles" of family therapy: *Conjoint Family Therapy* and *Peoplemaking*

Dione Sommers, Ph.D.: clinical psychologist; coordinator of annual Mother-Daughter Day at UCLA; mother of a grown daughter

Karen Speros: school counselor; teacher (recently voted Orange County teacher of the year); co-director, Crossroads Peer Counseling; mother of a teenage daughter and son

Judith Stevens-Long, Ph.D.: associate professor of psychology, California State University at Los Angeles; active in work with mother-daughter dyads; author of a professional paper on the subject called "Dependence vs. Independence"

Gary Strokosh, M.D.: director, clinic for adolescent medicine, Rush-Presbyterian Hospital, Chicago, Illinois

Joseph Teicher, M.D.: director of child and adolescent psychiatry, Los Angeles County–USC Medical Center

Marty Wasserman, Ph.D.: chief clinical psychologist and director of "Hotline," Children's Hospital of Los Angeles

Gordon Yeaton: counselor, teacher, co-director of Crossroads Peer Counseling, Irvine, California

Carol Zimmerman: executive director and counselor, New Directions for Young Women, Tucson, Arizona

I am also deeply appreciative to the following individuals, organizations, and agencies, public and private, who kindly furnished me with information and direction.

The American Bar Association

The California Alliance Concerned With School-Age Parents

Josephina J. Card, Ph.D., of the American Institutes for Research in the Behavioral Sciences, Palo Alto, California, and Washington, D.C.

Care Manor Hospital, Adolescent Program for Drug and Alcohol Abuse, Orange, California

Gallup Youth Survey (Associated Press Newsfeatures)

Girls' Clubs of America, Inc.

The Alan Guttmacher Institute, Research and Development Division, Washington, D.C.

Johns Hopkins Center for School-Aged Mothers and Their Infants, Johns Hopkins Medical Institutions, Baltimore, Maryland

The National Parents and Teachers Organization, Chicago

New Directions for Young Women, Tucson, Arizona

Odyssey Institute, Inc., New York, New York

Parents Without Partners, Inc., Washington, D.C.

Planned Parenthood Federation of America, Inc., New York, New York

The Population Institute, Washington, D.C.

Project Teen Concern, Planned Parenthood of Alameda-San Francisco

Dr. Patricia Schiller, M.A., J.D.: executive director, American Association of Sex Educators, Counselors and Therapists, Washington, D.C.

The Society for Adolescent Medicine, Granada Hills, California

The United States Department of Health, Education and Welfare:
Administration for Children, Youth and Families
Alcohol, Drug Abuse, and Mental Health Administration
Office of Human Development Services
Office on Smoking and Health

The United States Office of Education: Interagency Task Force on Comprehensive Programs for School-Age Parents

The United States Office of Juvenile Justice and Delinquency Prevention

The Urban Institute: Programs of Research on Women and Family Policy, Washington, D.C.